# Hovercraft and Hydrofoils

## in Colour

*Roy McLeavy*

# Hovercraft
# and Hydrofoils

## in Colour

*Illustrated by*

John W. Wood
E. Bruce
B. Hiley
J. Pelling

**BLANDFORD PRESS**

Poole        Dorset

Blandford Press Ltd
Link House, West Street,
Poole, Dorset BH15 1LL
First published 1976
Copyright © 1976 Blandford Press Ltd
ISBN 0 7137 0767 4

Set in 10/11 Baskerville
by Woolaston Parker Limited, Leicester
Printed and bound by
Richard Clay (Chaucer Press)
Bungay Suffolk

Colour Plates by Colour Reproductions, Billericay

# CONTENTS

# ACKNOWLEDGEMENTS

The author would like to express his indebtedness to the many members of the ACV and hydrofoil industries who made this book possible. Particular thanks are due to Neil MacDonald, who so kindly checked the ACV references; to Baron Hanns von Schertel, on whose excellent papers much of the historical background has been based; to Christopher and Nadia Hook for their interest and encouragement; to Tom Milton, Washington, D.C. and to W. A. Graig (better known as Grunberg—the name he used in his pioneering days) for his guidance on some of the fundamentals of foil design.

A special 'thank-you' also to Herbert Snowball who has contributed immeasurably to the author's knowledge of the subject by inviting him to assist in the operation of Airavia Ltd and Speed Hydrofoils.

Among other 'mentors' to whom acknowledgements are gratefully made are Leslie Colquhoun, Robert Trillo, Eugene Liberatore, Rowland Hunt, Dr Alexander Lippisch, Volker Jost and Eugen Schatté.

Those two mainstays of industry news and critique—*Hovering Craft & Hydrofoil* and *Hoverfoil News*—proved, as always, invaluable references, and not surprisingly perhaps, frequent forays were made into the pages of *Jane's Surface Skimmers*.

Other sources which added a great deal to the manuscript are: *Hydrofoils*, by Christopher Hook and A. C. Kermode, Sir Isaac Pitman & Sons Ltd, and *Hovercraft Design and Construction*, by G. H. Elsley and A. J. Devereaux, David & Charles, Newton Abbott.

Technical papers referred to in the course of preparing the text included 'Jets, Props and Air Cushions: Propulsion Technology and Surface Effect Ships', by Alfred Skolnick and Z. G. Wachnik of the Surface Effect Ships Project Office; 'The Development of Automatic Control Systems for Hydrofoil Craft', by R. L. Johnston and W. C. O'Neill; 'Powering Systems for Advanced Surface Vehicles', by George Rosen and G. R. Ketley, and 'Hovercraft Skirts', by R. C. Wheeler, British Hovercraft Corporation. The last three papers were presented at the International Hovering Craft, Hydrofoil and Advanced Transit Systems Conference at Brighton in May 1974.

The colour photograph on the back of the jacket has been reproduced by kind permission of Hoverlloyd Ltd., and the Royal Navy.

Finally the author would like to acknowledge the tremendous assistance given by Terry Goldsmith and Barry Gregory of Blandford Press; by Shirley and Sara McLeavy for typing the manuscript, and by Jack Wood and his team whose superb illustrations present so vivid a picture of the vessels that are beginning to open a fresh chapter in the saga of the sea.

# FOREWORD

Since the beginning of recorded history, the only craft to ply the waters of the world have been those kept afloat by Archimedes' displacement principle—that an object partially or totally immersed in a fluid is buoyed up or sustained by a force equal to the weight of the fluid displaced.

The art of shipbuilding has been one of the slowest to progress, even in modern times, and while displacement vessels have proved rugged, buoyant and stable, the frictional resistance they encounter, due to the density of the water through which they have to propel their hulls, places them among the least efficient means of transport known to man.

Today, sea transportation is undergoing a vigorous re-birth. We live in a changing world in which science, technology and economics play an increasingly dominant part. The modern shipowner, in his quest for higher performance, greater reliability, easier maintenance, smaller crews and improved profitability, is turning increasingly to non-displacement craft. Gradually, the 2,000 year-old discovery of Archimedes is being circumvented by vessels employing Sir Christopher Cockerell's hovercraft principle and Dr Daniel Bernoulli's principle of dynamic lift. It is to this new generation of high-speed passenger craft and load carriers, which skim across sea or land at interface level, that this book is dedicated.

The pages that follow tell the story, in abbreviated form, of some of the more important developments that have taken place in the evolution of the surface skimmers, as well as who was involved, and when and where the various designs were developed. Also described in the book are the duties many of the craft perform and the intricate machinery and systems that set them in motion. Written for the non-specialist and younger reader, it is hoped that it will encourage further interest in the new technology, thus helping to widen its acceptance, particularly among those looking to sea for their future profession.

Old shellbacks who survived the transition from sail to steam showed their contempt for the latter by telling former shipmates they were 'leaving the sea and going into steam'. Today, perhaps, for 'steam' they would substitute 'flying'. If so, they could hardly argue about the sturdy, lightweight construction of the fast new 'zero draft' craft, their compact controls and instrumentation, and the comfort of the crew compartments and passenger saloons. Nor could they complain about their conditions or pay.

Equally, with their keen eye for the shipshape, they would find it hard to take exception to the appearance of the new vessels. Name any of them—BH.7s, SR.N6s, RHS 160s, Kometas, PTS 75s, PHMs, Jetfoils, PP-15s. Each and every one built with graceful, flowing lines and boasting a performance to match! Even the square-lined SR.N4 has an efficient, purposeful appearance—and who could fail to be impressed with a ferry that carries payloads of more than 80 tons across a major waterway at speeds which have exceeded 70 knots?

Although the book has been written chiefly for those interested in the future of sea transport, pages are also devoted to various other areas of 'skimmer' technology. The air-cushion principle is being applied to 300 mph inter-city trains as well as to hovertrailers and giant hoverplatforms, designed to traverse marshy and ice-bound terrain. A direct descendant of the hovercraft skirt system is the industrial skirt, which is being employed throughout the world to move a variety of heavy loads, including the oil industry's biggest storage tanks.

Finally, apart from the fast, cushion-borne Aerofoil Boats and Ekranoplans, there is a new generation of giant cargo planes which will employ air-cushion landing systems to enable them to operate from both land and water.

Perhaps in view of all the current efforts to bring speed and comfort to travel at sea, the old shellbacks would have approved after all, just as we hope their descendants do. The revolution at sea is just beginning and the pages within simply mark the prelude. The early generation craft have proved the concepts and point the way to the future. Through them we can already discern the shape of the incredibly fast merchantmen and men-of-war of tomorrow.

Roy McLeavy

# THE COLOUR PLATES

## FIRST OFF

*Above:* Enrico Forlanini, the Italian airship and helicopter pioneer, built the world's first successful manned hydrofoil – the 38-knot ladder-foiled 'Hydro-Aeroplane' – in 1905.
*Below:* First practical sidewall air-cushion vehicle was this 40-knot torpedo-boat designed and built for the Austrian Navy in 1916 by Herr Dagobert Muller von Thomamhul.

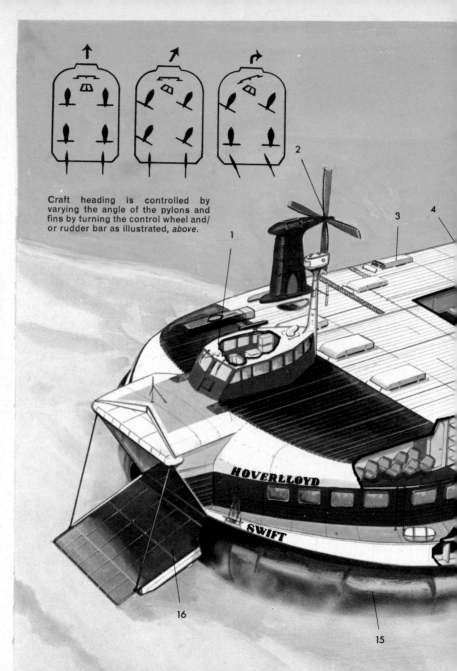

Craft heading is controlled by varying the angle of the pylons and fins by turning the control wheel and/ or rudder bar as illustrated, *above*.

With an all-up weight of 200 tons and a cruising speed of 60 knots, the **SR.N4 Mountbatten** is one of the largest and fastest amphibious hovercraft in the world. In standard configuration these craft carry 254 passengers and 30 vehicles.

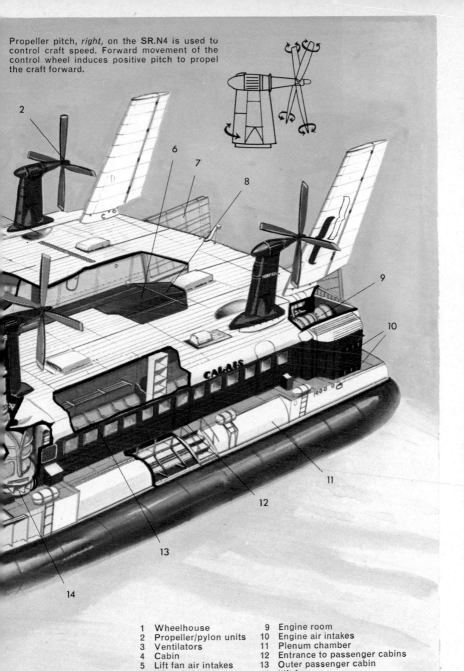

Propeller pitch, *right,* on the SR.N4 is used to control craft speed. Forward movement of the control wheel induces positive pitch to propel the craft forward.

| | | | |
|---|---|---|---|
| 1 | Wheelhouse | 9 | Engine room |
| 2 | Propeller/pylon units | 10 | Engine air intakes |
| 3 | Ventilators | 11 | Plenum chamber |
| 4 | Cabin | 12 | Entrance to passenger cabins |
| 5 | Lift fan air intakes | 13 | Outer passenger cabin |
| 6 | Car deck | 14 | Lift fan |
| 7 | Rear door | 15 | Skirt |
| 8 | Loading ramp | 16 | Bow door/ramp |

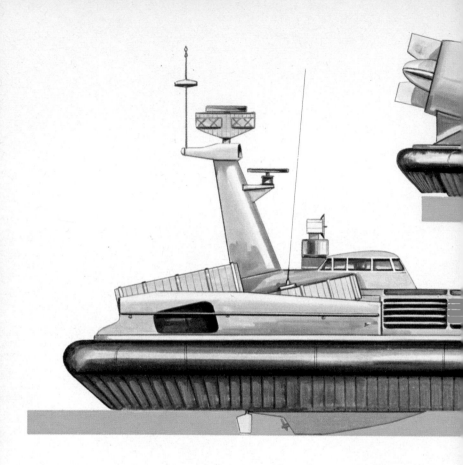

*Above:* A 100-ton fast patrol boat based on the VT 1. Unlike the air-propelled VT 2, the earlier VT 1 derives its thrust from two skeg-mounted water propellers, driven via Vee-drive gearboxes. Craft direction is controlled by twin water rudders and varying the pitch of the two propellers.

*Right:* Missile-equipped fast patrol version of the VT 2. Maximum speed is 60 knots.

Vosper Thornycroft's VT 2 equipped for patrol duties.

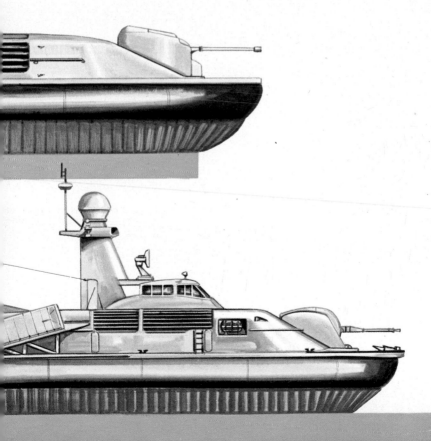

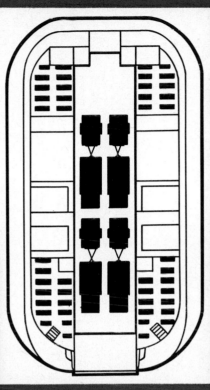

The prototype VT 2 is capable of carrying a company of 130 fully-armed troops and their vehicles. With the entrance ramp and deck reinforced, it can carry a 50-ton Chieftain tank. If required, the craft could be deployed from the United Kingdom to any point on the coast of Europe or the Mediterranean under its own power. Power is supplied by two 4,500 shp Proteus gas-turbines, each of which drives a bank of four centrifugal lift fans and a ducted propulsion fan.

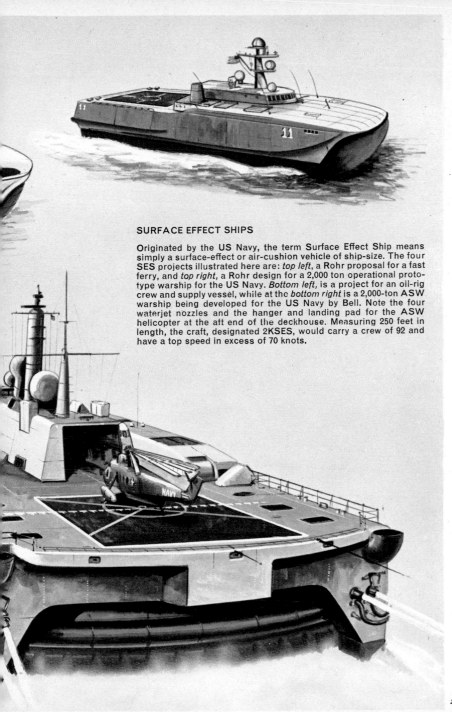

## SURFACE EFFECT SHIPS

Originated by the US Navy, the term Surface Effect Ship means simply a surface-effect or air-cushion vehicle of ship-size. The four SES projects illustrated here are: *top left*, a Rohr proposal for a fast ferry, and *top right,* a Rohr design for a 2,000 ton operational proto-type warship for the US Navy. *Bottom left,* is a project for an oil-rig crew and supply vessel, while at the *bottom right,* is a 2,000-ton ASW warship being developed for the US Navy by Bell. Note the four waterjet nozzles and the hanger and landing pad for the ASW helicopter at the aft end of the deckhouse. Measuring 250 feet in length, the craft, designated 2KSES, would carry a crew of 92 and have a top speed in excess of 70 knots.

Japan's biggest production hovercraft is the 155-seat Mitsui MV-PP15, which has a service speed about 50 knots (app. 90 km/h). Motive power is provided by two 1,950 hp Avco Lycoming TF 25 gas turbines each driving a thirteen-bladed centrifugal fan for lift and a four-bladed variable-pitch propeller for thrust. Craft heading is controlled by twin aerodynamic rudders in the propeller slipstream and differential propeller thrust.

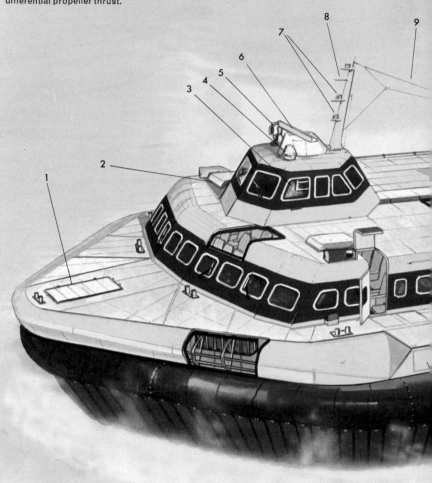

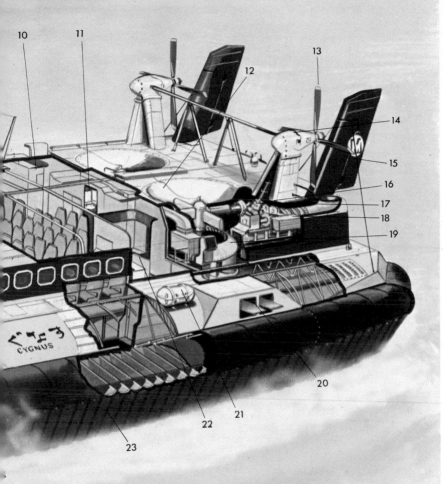

| | | | | | |
|---|---|---|---|---|---|
| 1 | Anchor locker | 9 | Radio aerial | 17 | Main gearbox |
| 2 | Cabin air duct | 10 | Luggage space | 18 | Gas-turbine |
| 3 | Flight deck | 11 | WC/washbasin unit | 19 | Lift fan |
| 4 | Searchlight | 12 | Fan air intake | 20 | Aft thrust port |
| 5 | Electric horn | 13 | Propeller for thrust | 21 | Inflatable liferaft |
| 6 | Radar | 14 | Propeller gearbox | 22 | Bar |
| 7 | Navigation light | 15 | Aerodynamic rudder | 23 | Flexible fingered-bag type skirt |
| 8 | Pitot tubo | 16 | Fan gearbox | 24 | Bow thrust port |

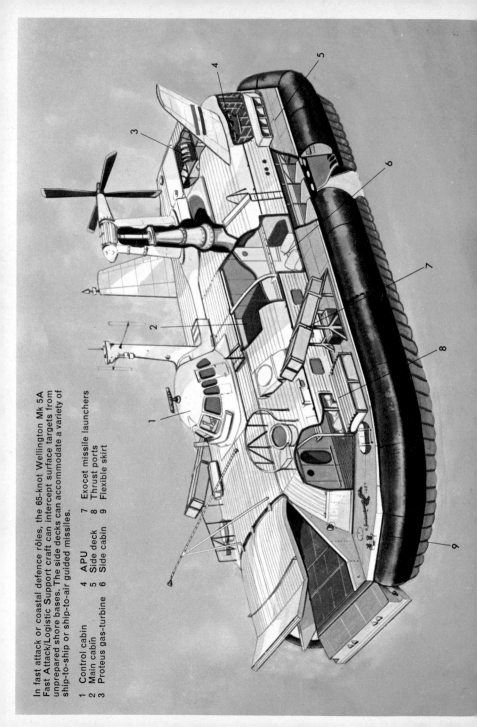

In fast attack or coastal defence rôles, the 65-knot Wellington Mk 5A Fast Attack/Logistic Support craft can intercept surface targets from unprepared shore bases. The side decks can accommodate a variety of ship-to-ship or ship-to-air guided missiles.

1 Control cabin
2 Main cabin
3 Proteus gas-turbine
4 APU
5 Side deck
6 Side cabin
7 Exocet missile launchers
8 Thrust ports
9 Flexible skirt

# SES TEST CRAFT

Aerojet-General Corporation's SES-100A test craft, built to assist the US Navy to determine the feasibility of operating large, fast, surface effect ships of 4,000-5,000 tons and capable of 80 knots or more.

1 Engine air inlets

2 Axial-flow fan

3 Bridge

4 Stabilizer

5 Movable skeg, employed for directional control at high speed.

6 One of four, 3,500 shp Avco Lycoming gas-turbines. The transmission system couples the gas-turbines to two axial/centrifugal waterjet pumps and three axial-flow lift fans.

7 Waterjet pump inlet

8 Engine exhaust

9 Fan air inlets

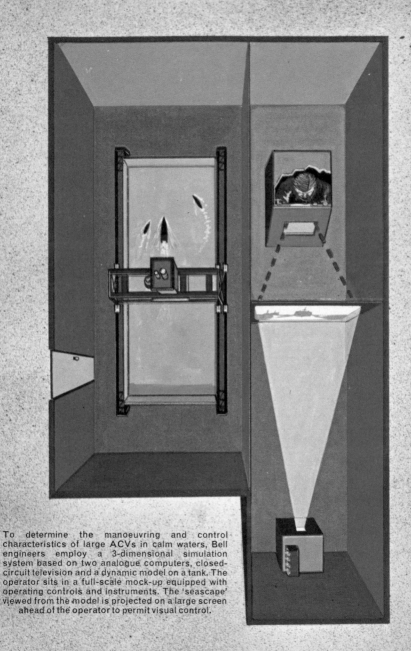

To determine the manoeuvring and control characteristics of large ACVs in calm waters, Bell engineers employ a 3-dimensional simulation system based on two analogue computers, closed-circuit television and a dynamic model on a tank. The operator sits in a full-scale mock-up equipped with operating controls and instruments. The 'seascape' viewed from the model is projected on a large screen ahead of the operator to permit visual control.

1 Tubular pontoon

2 Fuel tank

3 Nacelle housing generator

4 Wing connecting tubular pontoons

5 One of two aft inverted V foils.

6 Boom with sweep cables attached

7 One of two bow foils of surface-piercing, tandem foil system

8 Pitch control subfoil

9 Towing bridle

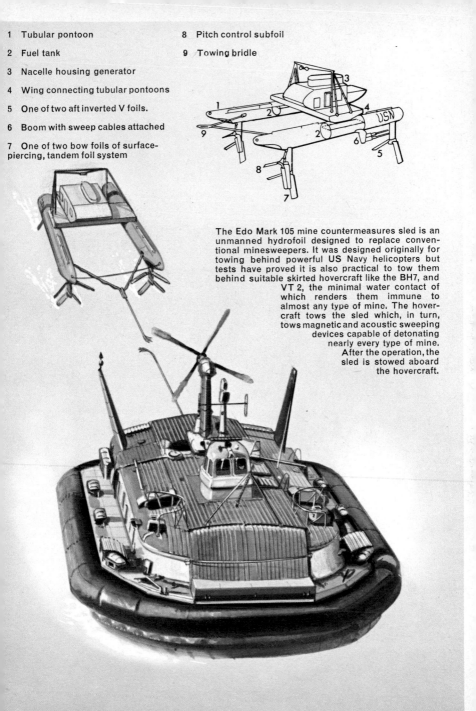

The Edo Mark 105 mine countermeasures sled is an unmanned hydrofoil designed to replace conventional minesweepers. It was designed originally for towing behind powerful US Navy helicopters but tests have proved it is also practical to tow them behind suitable skirted hovercraft like the BH7, and VT 2, the minimal water contact of which renders them immune to almost any type of mine. The hovercraft tows the sled which, in turn, tows magnetic and acoustic sweeping devices capable of detonating nearly every type of mine. After the operation, the sled is stowed aboard the hovercraft.

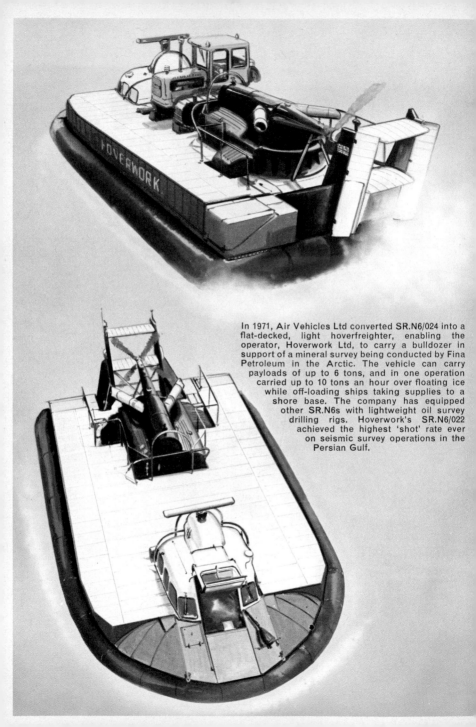

In 1971, Air Vehicles Ltd converted SR.N6/024 into a flat-decked, light hoverfreighter, enabling the operator, Hoverwork Ltd, to carry a bulldozer in support of a mineral survey being conducted by Fina Petroleum in the Arctic. The vehicle can carry payloads of up to 6 tons, and in one operation carried up to 10 tons an hour over floating ice while off-loading ships taking supplies to a shore base. The company has equipped other SR.N6s with lightweight oil survey drilling rigs. Hoverwork's SR.N6/022 achieved the highest 'shot' rate ever on seismic survey operations in the Persian Gulf.

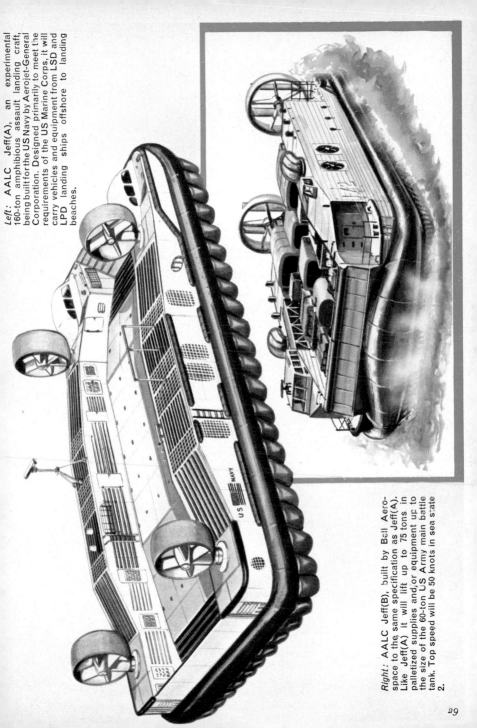

*Left:* AALC Jeff(A), an experimental 160-ton amphibious assault landing craft, being built for the US Navy by Aerojet-General Corporation. Designed primarily to meet the requirements of the US Marine Corps, it will carry vehicles and equipment from LSD and LPD landing ships offshore to landing beaches.

*Right:* AALC Jeff(B), built by Bell Aerospace to the same specification as Jeff(A). Like Jeff(A) it will lift up to 75 tons in palletized supplies and/or equipment up to the size of the 60-ton US Army main battle tank. Top speed will be 50 knots in sea state 2.

The basic
Voyageur hard
structure breaks down into
twelve major sections. The
modules are the three forward flotation
boxes, two forward and two aft sidedecks,
two power modules, an aft centre flotation box, cabin
support pedestal and the central cabin.

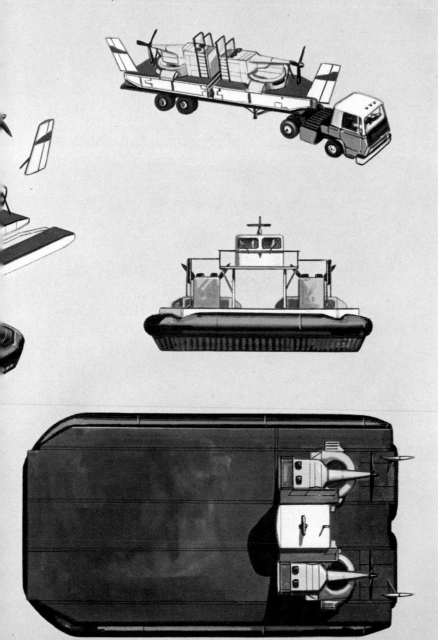

Bell Canada's ruggedly-built Voyageur, a 65-ft long amphibious multi-duty hovercraft, is now the accepted ACV 'workhorse' of the American and Canadian Far North. It hauls payloads of up to 25 tons across ice and snow at 50 m.p.h.

Amphibious hovercraft are regarded as the only vehicles likely to assist in the rapid development of the Arctic regions of Alaska, Canada and the Soviet Union.

One of two SR.N6s, *above*, used by Northern Transportation Co for charter operations including seismographic and hydrographic surveys and logistic support to offshore oil rigs.

Voyageurs, *above*, have proved to be five times faster than conventional lighters and have the ability to land containers at points inland. Normal off-loading facilities are not necessary.

A Voyageur, *above,* operated by Northern Transportation Co., equipped to lay cable from a 17-ton reel.

A concept by Bell Aerospace for a 150-ton, 80-knot Arctic SEV, *above,* based on the engines, systems and components of AALC Jeff(B).

In 1970, a Royal Navy BH.7 carried firemen and a medical team to the tanker Pacific Glory, which caught fire off the Isle of Wight, and assisted the search for missing seamen. Hovercraft have often been called out to rescue crews of burning ships.

The ACV is potentially the fastest vessel available for the inspection of buoys and lighthouses, *above*.

Many search and rescue operations call for the relief of occupants of light craft that have run aground, *right*.

During an eighteen month evaluation of ACVs by the US Coast Guard, three 70-knot Bell SK-5s (license-built SR.N5s) proved that ACVs could provide a more effective response capability at less cost.

The Air Vehicles Ltd AV.2, *left*
two converted outboard engines

A Cushioncraft CC.7 light utility hovercraft. Two centrifugal fans, driven by a single 390 hp STB60 gas-turbine, provide the pressurised air for both lift and thrust.

ngined 5-6 seater, powered by
ble of 35 knots.

Sealand Hovercraft of Millom, Cumbria, is the builder of the SH-2, *above*, an elegant six-seater designed for duties ranging from water-taxi and ambulance to patrol craft.

The combination hovercraft/aerosleds, *above* and *below*, were built by Finnish designer Erkki Peri to operate in snow, ice and floods in northern latitudes. Because of the contact between the vehicle's buoyant, pontoon-type skis and the supporting surface below, the driver has more positive directional control when operating over snow and ice than with a skirted ACV. The forward ski/pontoons and the air rudder move simultaneously to control craft heading.

*Above:* Rear view of the Peri Hoversled 1.

rst hovercraft of Italian design to go into production was
e BT.4–74, *above*, a three-seater designed by Captain Tito
ettocchi of the Italian Air Force.

mong the operators of the Air Bearings Crossbow is the Nigerian Police
orce, *above*. Triple rudders operating in the airjet exit provide directional
ontrol. Reverse thrust is by a shutter and vane system.

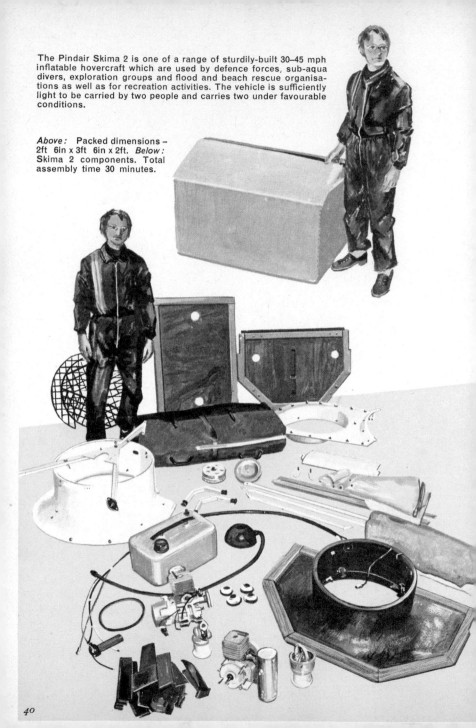

The Pindair Skima 2 is one of a range of sturdily-built 30–45 mph inflatable hovercraft which are used by defence forces, sub-aqua divers, exploration groups and flood and beach rescue organisations as well as for recreation activities. The vehicle is sufficiently light to be carried by two people and carries two under favourable conditions.

*Above:* Packed dimensions – 2ft 6in x 3ft 6in x 2ft. *Below:* Skima 2 components. Total assembly time 30 minutes.

# Conditions to be Observed by the Holder of this Ticket

1. This Ticket shall only be available to the party in whose favour it is granted, and it is *not transferable.*

2. The holder of this ticket will have the privilege of fishing with a single rod and line, on week days only, during the period mentioned hereon but the holder MUST NOT KILL ANY TROUT UNDER EIGHT INCHES IN LENGTH, OR ANY SMOLTS OR PARR.

3. **No Minnow Fishing, Spinning, Ground Baiting, Float Fishing, Fixed Spools or Multi Ply Reels Allowed.**

4. The holder of this ticket must exhibit it to the Association Watchers or other persons having authority to demand exhibition thereof, at all times when asked to do so, and any person refusing or failing to exhibit this ticket may be turned off the river, and the ticket forfeited.

5. The holder of this ticket undertakes to fish with legal lures only, and to give all the assistance in his power to prevent illegal fishing and poaching. It shall be his duty at once to report all illegal acts to the Secretary or Watchers and he shall allow the Watchers or other persons duly authorised to inspect the fish and tackle in his possession.

6. No ticket-holder shall be accompanied by a dog.

7. Ticket-holders are requested to close all gates through which they pass and to avoid damaging fences or other property or disturbing game.

8. The fishing season shall commence on 1st April and shall terminate on 30th September.

9. Leaving of litter, particularly broken glass, is prohibited.

10. Any holder of a ticket infringing any of the foregoing Rules and Regulations shall forfeit his ticket and the leave granted will at once cease. Such forfeiture shall be at once caused by a letter under the hand of the Secretary of the Association, directed to the ticket-holder at the address stated in his ticket.

11. Any member who has been convicted of a breach of the Tweed Fisheries Acts or the Fresh Water Fisheries Acts then in force or who takes any fish by other means than by rod and line and legal lure or who the Committee are satisfied has fished in any of the reserved stretches shall thereupon cease to be a member of the Association and shall not be re-admitted for a year from the date of the offence. A ticket-holder convicted of an offence under the above Acts shall at once surrender his ticket and shall not be granted another for at least one year from the date of such conviction.

12. The Association reserve the right to refuse membership to any person.

13. **The holder must at all times give way to Salmon Fishers.**

*Note.* — Members are requested to pay special attention to these Rules and to see that they are duly observed.

---

Holder's
Name ...........................................................

# N⁰ 3566

## GALA ANGLING ASSOCIATION

Name ..................................................

18/9/82 ...........Date

THIS TICKET allows holder to fish for Trout only on Association water as defined by notice boards.

**No Spinning or Minnow Fishing allowed.**

VISITORS' DAILY ... ...
(Monday–Friday).

VISITORS' WEEKLY ... ...

VISITORS' FORTNIGHTLY ...

VISITORS' SEASON ... ...

Received £ 1 : 00

Name .......................................

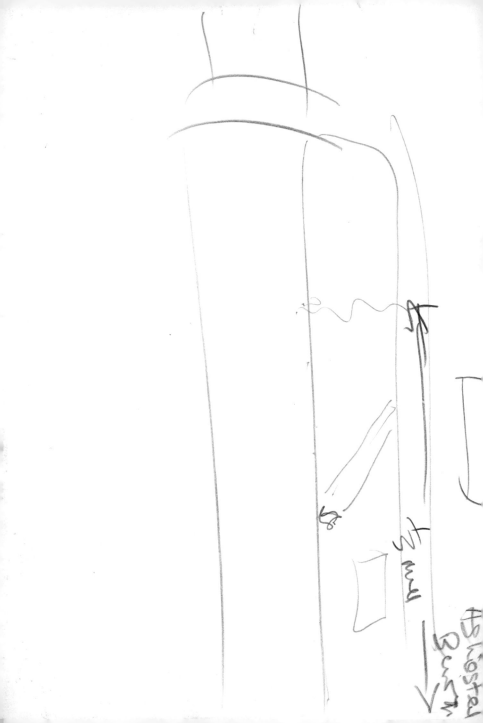

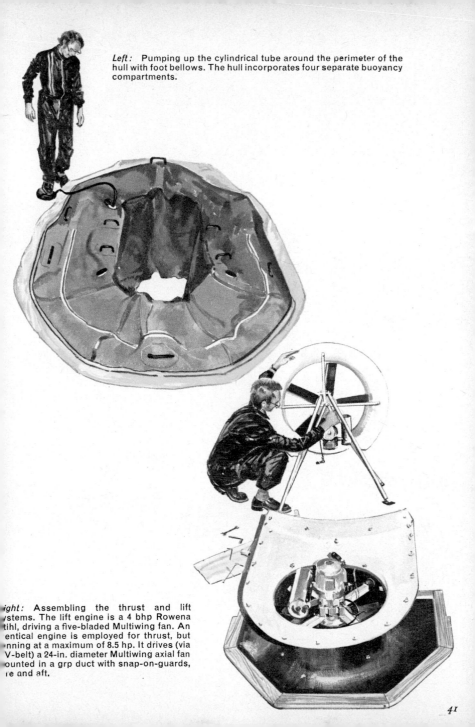

*Left:* Pumping up the cylindrical tube around the perimeter of the hull with foot bellows. The hull incorporates four separate buoyancy compartments.

*Right:* Assembling the thrust and lift systems. The lift engine is a 4 bhp Rowena Stihl, driving a five-bladed Multiwing fan. An identical engine is employed for thrust, but running at a maximum of 8.5 hp. It drives (via V-belt) a 24-in. diameter Multiwing axial fan mounted in a grp duct with snap-on-guards, fore and aft.

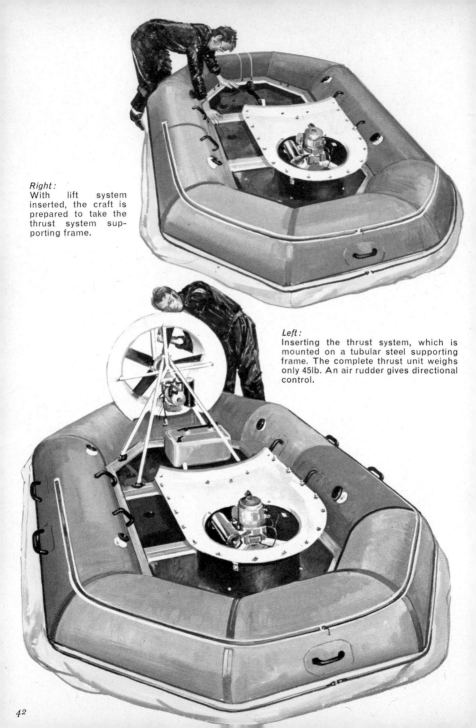

*Right:*
With lift system inserted, the craft is prepared to take the thrust system supporting frame.

*Left:*
Inserting the thrust system, which is mounted on a tubular steel supporting frame. The complete thrust unit weighs only 45lb. An air rudder gives directional control.

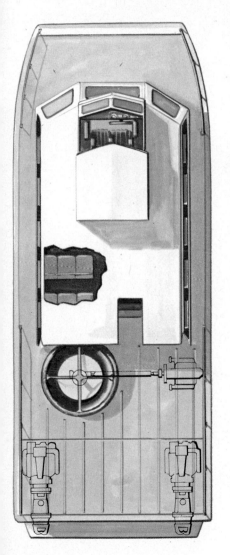

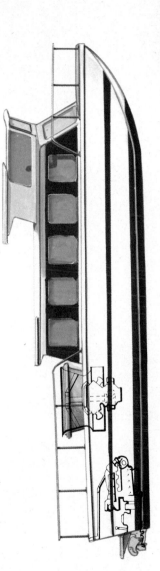

A product of Aircushion Boat Co of Tacoma, Washington, the Airboat is an air-cushion-assisted catamaran. The 42-ft Airboat illustrated is a passenger ferry/freighter seating twenty-one passengers. It has a top speed of 35 knots. Power is supplied by three GMC 6V-53 ciesels, one of which drives a large centrifugal fan aft of the deckhouse, while the remaining two, both supercharged and developing 250 hp, drive two Hamilton waterjets.

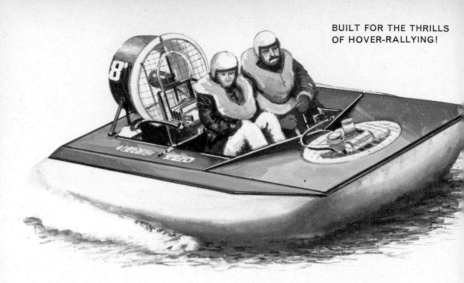

*Above:* 'Scarab Two' a 35 mph amphibious two-seater
built by G. Nutt, G. Brass and J. Lyne.

Amateur hovercraft builders in the UK, supported by British Petroleum, have introduced
Hover Rallying, the first-ever sport for amphibious speedsters.

*Above:* Aggro, a single-seater built by Messrs T. & T.
Wilcox of East Howe, Bournemouth, has an empty weight
of 400 lb and achieves 30 mph over water.

*Above:* During Hover Club speed trials in Scotland, Dair-e-Goes, a fibreglass-hulled two-seater, attained 37 mph over the measured mile. It was built by the staff of Job's Dairy, Hanworth, Middlesex.

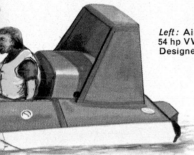

*Left:* Air-Lubri-Cat 4, a two-three seater powered by a 54 hp VW 1500 cc engine, *above,* has non-rigid sidewalls Designer is Derek Burnes of Rackheath, Norwich.

Riding on their air cushions, free of surface contact, sudden cross winds cause the craft to waltz sideways and drift wide of turns.

*Right:* Skyboy, a single-seater of wooden construction built by Robert Hull of Bramley, Nr. Basingstoke.

*Above:* Wasp an ultra light runabout built by Light Hovercraft Co.

*Above:* Hoverking's Ranger 1, a 55 m.p.h. single-seater. Winner of the 1973 United Kingdo
Hovercraft of the Year Award.

*Right:* Brazil's first light hovercraft
is the FE1 VA, a two-seater powered
by a Volkswagen engine.

*Below:* Built in Canada by Gordon Komar, the Aquaterra 65T has achieved 60 mph over ice.

*Below:* Aero Sabre Mk 1, a high-performance hover-scooter.

*Above:* The Light Hovercraft Buzzard, easy to operate and maintain, is available in two- and four-seat versions.

*Left:* The tiny single-seater UH-10 was built in the USA by Universal Hovercraft of Redondo Beach, California.

*Below:* Another Canadian miniature runabout is the Hovertec Chinook. It can be carried on the roof of a family car.

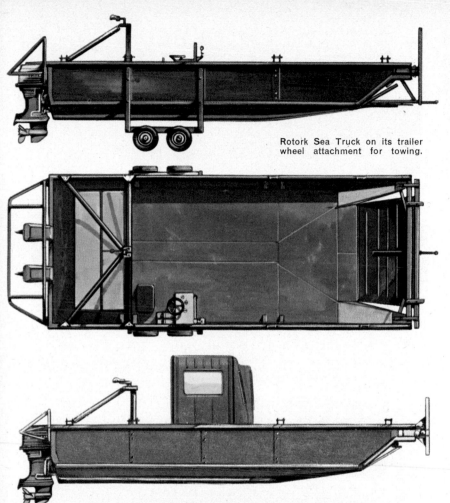

Rotork Sea Truck on its trailer wheel attachment for towing.

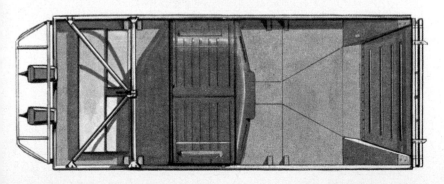

Sea Truck with a single modular cabin unit and twin outboard engines.

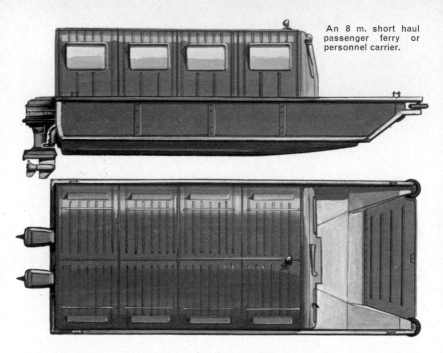

An 8 m. short haul passenger ferry or personnel carrier.

At speed, a ram-air cushion, contained by the shallow side skegs, raises the bow of the Sea Truch clear of the water. As the air flows aft, it mixes with water, providing air/foam lubrication for the rest of the hull, permitting speeds of up to 50 m.p.h. to be attained according to sea state and load.

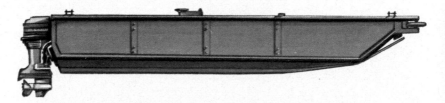

Rotork's 8 m. fast assault craft can operate in ankle depth water carrying up to thirty men.

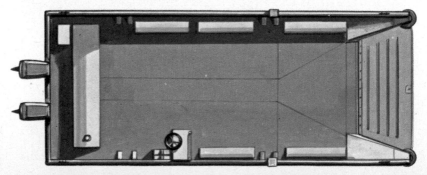

*Above:* Rotork 8 m. workboat or light vehicle ferry.
*Below:* Rotork general-purpose launch or fast patrol boat.

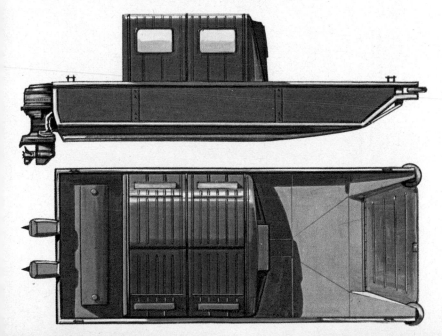

Zarya waterjet-propelled 65-seat water buses are in use throughout the Soviet Union on the many waterways which are too shallow for conventional craft and hydrofoils to navigate. As with British-built Rotork workboats, a localised ram-air cushion is generated at speed below the bow and contained by shallow skegs. As the air flows back beneath the flat bottomed hull, it provides air/foam lubrication. Powered by a single V-type diesel driving a single-stage water impeller, the Za.ya has a speed of 28 m.p.h. and can operate in channels only 20 in. deep. It seats 65 passengers.

# FOUR SKIMMERS FROM FRANCE

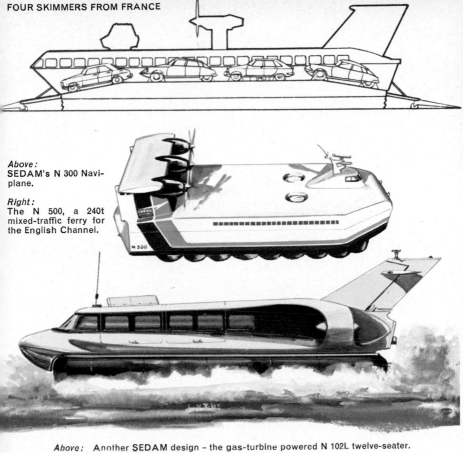

*Above:*
SEDAM's N 300 Navi-
plane.

*Right:*
The N 500, a 240t
mixed-traffic ferry for
the English Channel.

*Above:* Another SEDAM design – the gas-turbine powered N 102L twelve-seater.

*Below:* Aerospatiale's H 890, a 4-ton submerged foil test craft. The vessel has attained 50 knots during trials.

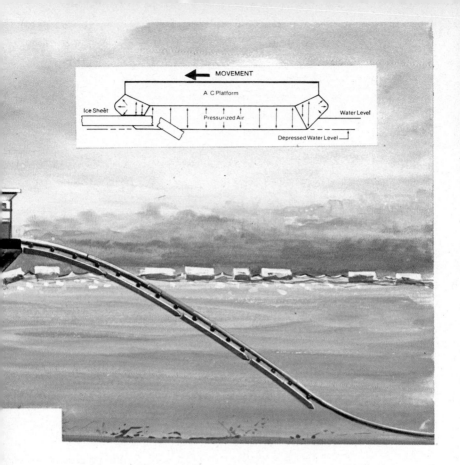

When Arctic Engineers & Constructors towed their ACT-100 air-cushion transporter across Arctic ice, they discovered they had created a novel form of icebreaker. Air in the pressurised zone beneath the craft depresses the water beneath the ice, which losing its support, cracks and falls into the displaced water below. One of the company's later concepts is an Arctic marine pipelaying vessel which combines the duty of ice-breaking with that of pipelaying. Conventional pipelaying vessels cannot operate in ice-bound waters.

The ACT-100 is an ACV barge built by Arctic Engineers & Constructors to support Arctic drill sites by carrying 100-ton payloads across tundra, muskeg and marsh without disturbing the soil and vegetation. It is either towed by tractors or can winch itself across the ice, pulling a cable attached to an anchor.

Designed for offshore use in the Arctic is this 3,840-ton Arctic drilling system, which combines an air-cushion-barge with a complete drilling rig. A hull heating system using waste heat from the engines melts ice drifting by to allow the vessel to float above the well bore.

*Above:* A Mackley-Ace hover platform in use by a construction company to make an offshore survey. The platforms are generally either winched or towed, although it is possible to propel them with outboard engines.

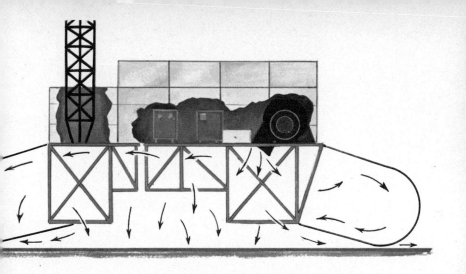

*Left:* First-ever oil-rig to be combined with an air-cushion platform was in use in the Soviet Union in 1967. The arrangement was the brainchild of a group of ACV engineers and designers headed by V. A. Shibanov. A standard BU-75 drilling rig is mounted on a rectangular all-metal buoyancy raft fitted with side structures to carry a flexible skirt. The drilling engines power the lift fans when the rig is being moved to a new site. Two tractors are used as tugs for the platform, which has an all-up weight of 170 tons.

*Above:* Much larger ACV rigs are under development in the Soviet Union. References have been made to hover platforms with load capacities of 'several thousand tons'.

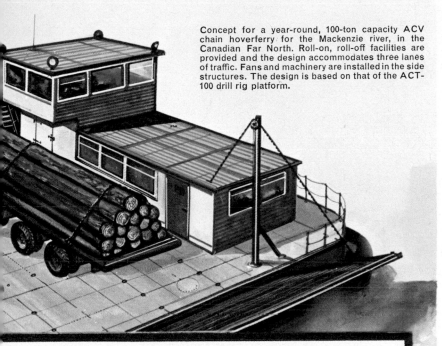

Concept for a year-round, 100-ton capacity ACV chain hoverferry for the Mackenzie river, in the Canadian Far North. Roll-on, roll-off facilities are provided and the design accommodates three lanes of traffic. Fans and machinery are installed in the side structures. The design is based on that of the ACT-100 drill rig platform.

The Canadian-designed Hover-Jak HJ.15 air-cushion trailer which has a Bertin multiple plenum lift system. Wheels fitted to swinging arms at the rear provide directional control on slopes and when reversing.

*Right:* This Sikorsky S-55 helicopter of Sky Rotors Ltd, proved the practicability of using a helicopter as a tug for the Hover-Jak HJ.15 in areas where it is necessary to limit damage in sensitive tundra.

*Below:* Sea Pearl, a 750-ton hover transporter built by Mackley-Ace to carry LNG plant modules from the fabrication site at Abu Dhabi to the installation site on Das Island, a distance of 110 miles.

A 30-ton capacity Mackley-Ace modular platform carrying a 28-ton dragline for offshore engineering work.

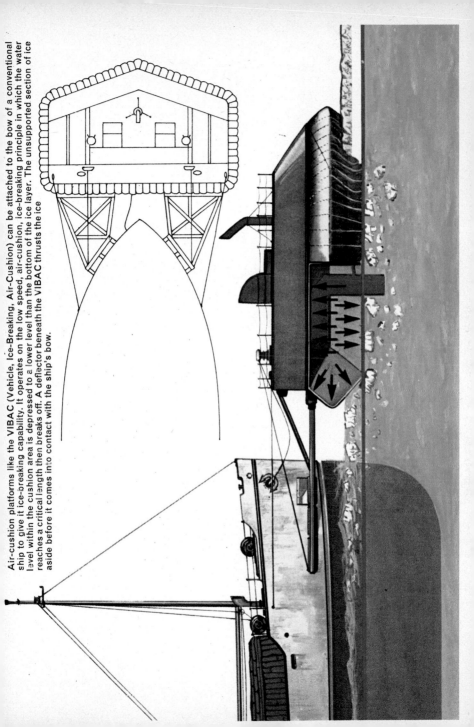

Air-cushion platforms like the VIBAC (Vehicle, Ice-Breaking, Air-Cushion) can be attached to the bow of a conventional ship to give it ice-breaking capability. It operates on the low speed, air-cushion, ice-breaking principle in which the water level within the cushion area is depressed to a lower level than the bottom of the ice layer. The unsupported section of ice reaches a critical length then breaks off. A deflector beneath the VIBAC thrusts the ice aside before it comes into contact with the ship's bow.

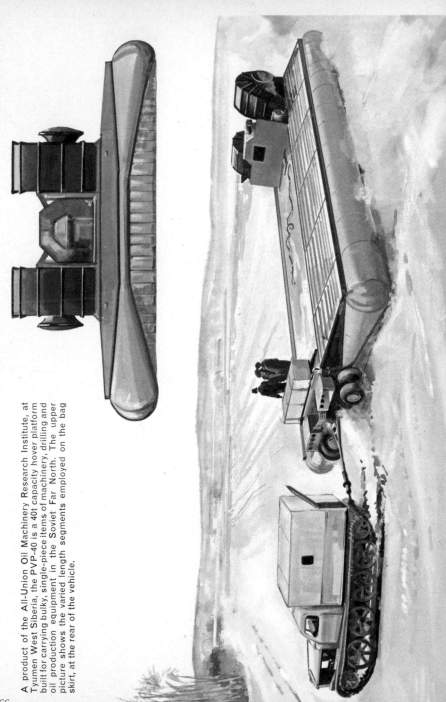

A product of the All-Union Oil Machinery Research Institute, at Tyumen West Siberia, the PVP-40 is a 40t capacity hover platform built for carrying bulky, single-piece items of machinery, drilling and oil production equipment in the Soviet Far North. The upper picture shows the varied length segments employed on the bag skirt, at the rear of the vehicle.

A Soviet combined ACV/crawler tractor and an air-cushion trailer designed for use in Siberian swamps to aid the petroleum and gas industries. The trailer, which weighs 7,700 lb. empty, can carry a payload of 13,200 lb. on its deck. The tractor, said to be capable of 50 m.p.h. over swamps, uses narrow caterpillar tracks for propulsion, steering and support on hard surfaces. The air-cushion is contained between the tracks by a flexible skirt.

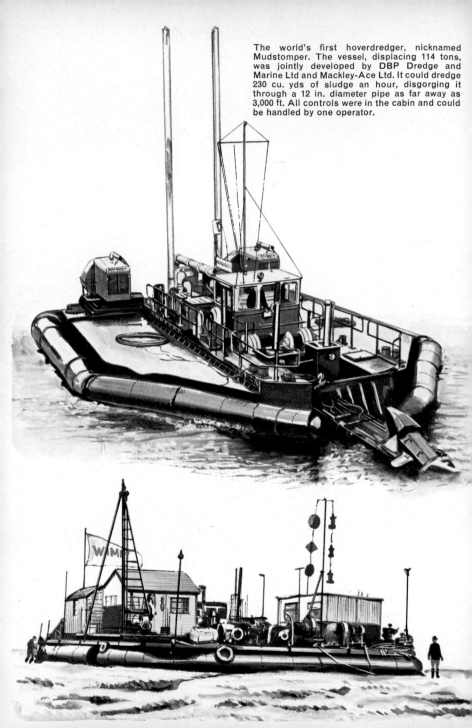

The world's first hoverdredger, nicknamed Mudstomper. The vessel, displacing 114 tons, was jointly developed by DBP Dredge and Marine Ltd and Mackley-Ace Ltd. It could dredge 230 cu. yds of sludge an hour, disgorging it through a 12 in. diameter pipe as far away as 3,000 ft. All controls were in the cabin and could be handled by one operator.

One of Dr Alexander M. Lippisch's delta-winged Aerofoil Boat concepts. Vehicles of this type are known as aerodynamic ACVs. Like aircraft, they depend upon forward speed to develop lift, then ride on a dynamic cushion of air which is set up between them and the supporting surface below. This particular vehicle has an all-up weight of six tons, is powered by a gas-turbine and will seat twenty-four passengers.

Stability of the X-113 Am is such that it can be flown in ground effect 'hands off'.

Projected 300-ton freighter with catamaran hull.

Lippisch X-112, powered by a 25 hp Richter drone engine.

## NEW FLYING-BOAT AGE

The Aerofoil Boats seen on this page fly low down in a ground effect cushion which results in a sharp decrease in their drag, lowers their fuel consumption and increases their load carrying capacity by as much as 400 per cent.

A design proposal for a 6-ton river bus.

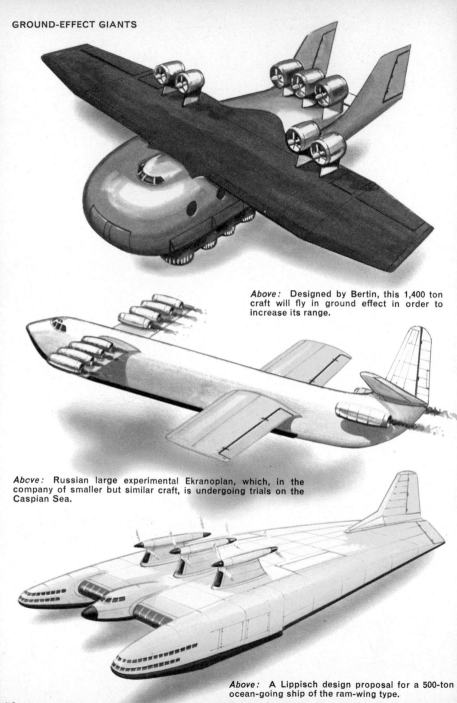

*Above:* Designed by Bertin, this 1,400 ton craft will fly in ground effect in order to increase its range.

*Abcve:* Russian large experimental Ekranoplan, which, in the company of smaller but similar craft, is undergoing trials on the Caspian Sea.

*Above:* A Lippisch design proposal for a 500-ton ocean-going ship of the ram-wing type.

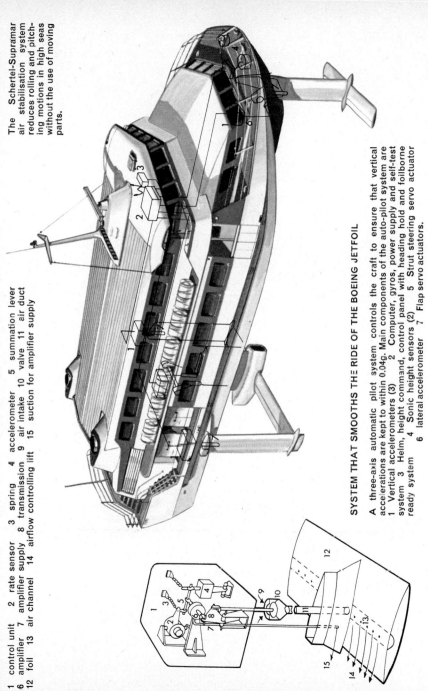

The Schertel-Supramar air stabilisation system reduces rolling and pitching motions in high seas without the use of moving parts.

## SYSTEM THAT SMOOTHS THE RIDE OF THE BOEING JETFOIL

A three-axis automatic pilot system controls the craft to ensure that vertical accelerations are kept to within 0.04g. Main components of the auto-pilot system are
1 Vertical accelerometers (3)    2 Computer, gyros, power supply and self-test system 3 Helm, height command, control panel with heading hold and foilborne ready system    4 Sonic height sensors (2)    5 Strut steering servo actuator
6 lateral accelerometer    7 Flap servo actuators.

1 control unit    2 rate sensor    3 spring    4 accelerometer    5 summation lever
6 amplifier    7 amplifier supply    8 transmission    9 air intake    10 valve    11 air duct
12 foil    13 air channel    14 airflow controlling lift    15 suction for amplifier supply

73

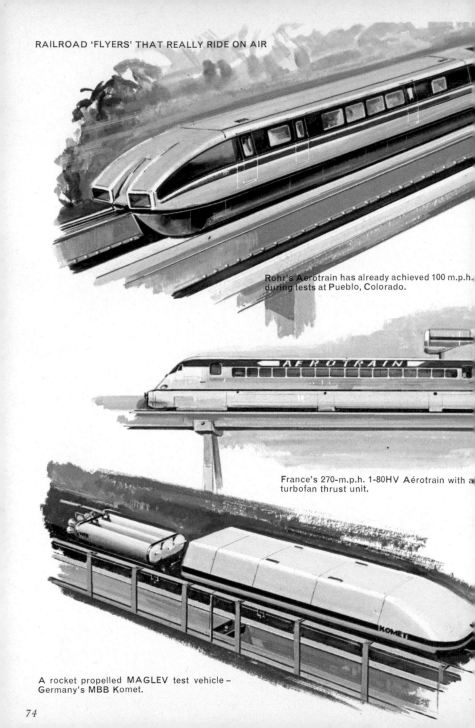

Rohr's Aerotrain has already achieved 100 m.p.h. during tests at Pueblo, Colorado.

France's 270-m.p.h. 1-80HV Aérotrain with a turbofan thrust unit.

A rocket propelled MAGLEV test vehicle – Germany's MBB Komet.

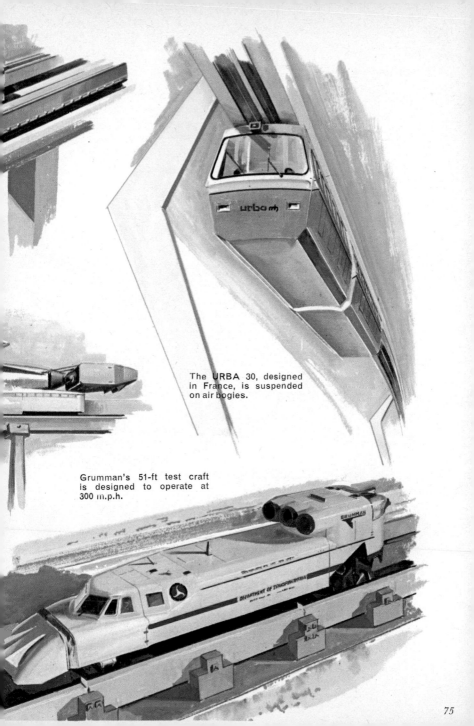

The URBA 30, designed in France, is suspended on air bogies.

Grumman's 51-ft test craft is designed to operate at 300 m.p.h.

# AIR CUSHIONS FOR SOFT LANDINGS

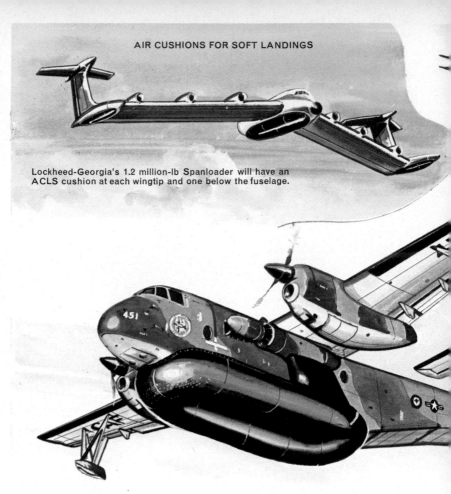

Lockheed-Georgia's 1.2 million-lb Spanloader will have an ACLS cushion at each wingtip and one below the fuselage.

First large aircraft to employ an ACLS is the XC-8A Buffalo.

Multiple air cushions were recommended for a multiterrain variant of the A-4 Skyhawk.

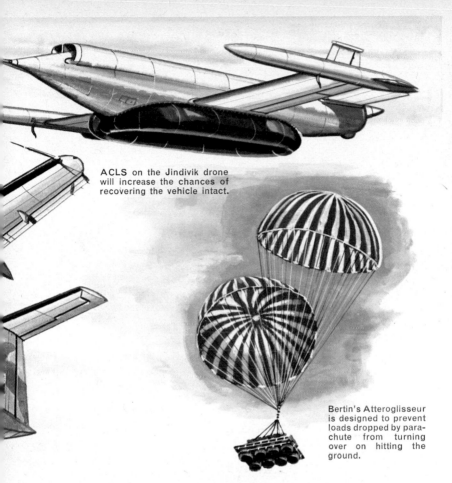

ACLS on the Jindivik drone will increase the chances of recovering the vehicle intact.

Bertin's Atteroglisseur is designed to prevent loads dropped by parachute from turning over on hitting the ground.

First aircraft, *below,* to prove the practicability of the ACLS was this modified Lake L–4.

First crossing of the Pacific by a hydrofoil sailboat was completed in September 1970 by Dave Keiper's Williwaw. A 31-ft trimaran, it has a V-foil at the bow, a ladder foil at the stern and one laterally outboard of each of the port and starboard pontoons. Top speed, in a strong steady wind, is 30 knots.

One of Christopher Hook's Sailing Hydrofin projects (*right*). Stability is maintained by sensors adjusting the incidence of the submerged foils.

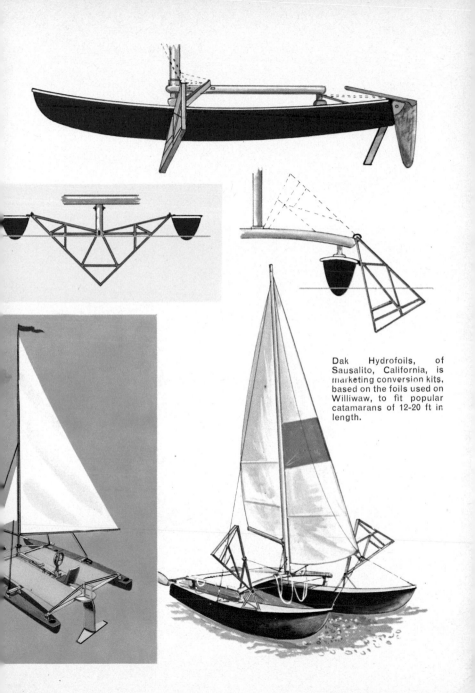

Dak Hydrofoils, of Sausalito, California, is marketing conversion kits, based on the foils used on Williwaw, to fit popular catamarans of 12-20 ft in length.

*Above:* RHS 110, a 54-ton hydrofoil ferry designed to carry up to 110 passengers.

*Right:* RHS Aliyacht, a luxury yacht with a speed of 38 knots and range of 400 miles.

*Below:* Condor 3, an RHS 1400 operated by Condor Ltd between the Channel Islands and France.

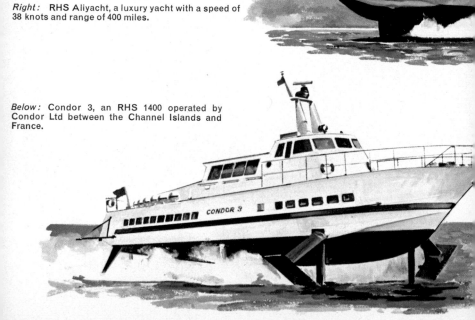

*Above:* Porto Corsini, an RHS 70 Hydrofoil off-shore drill platform supply vessel. It can carry a 3-ton load on its open deck

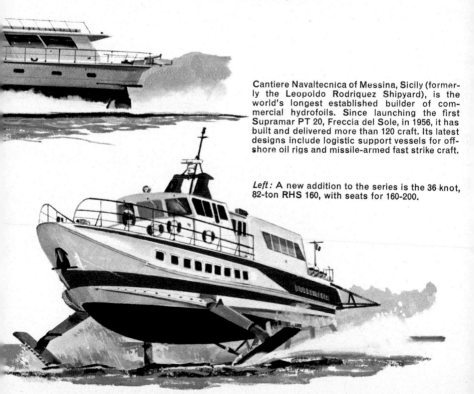

Cantiere Navaltecnica of Messina, Sicily (formerly the Leopoldo Rodriquez Shipyard), is the world's longest established builder of commercial hydrofoils. Since launching the first Supramar PT 20, Freccia del Sole, in 1956, it has built and delivered more than 120 craft. Its latest designs include logistic support vessels for off-shore oil rigs and missile-armed fast strike craft.

*Left:* A new addition to the series is the 36 knot, 82-ton RHS 160, with seats for 160-200.

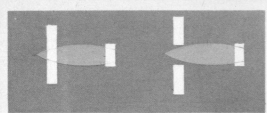

## BASIC FOIL CONFIGURATIONS

*Left:* Conventional or 'aeroplane' foil system. The main foil is sometimes split into two to permit retraction.

Tandem foil system, *right.* Area of the forward foils is roughly equivalent to that of the aft foils, the load being balanced between them.

*Left:* Canard foil arrangement with a wide span main foil located at the stern, aft of the centre of gravity, and a small foil at the bow.

Platforming – flying level over waves lower than the calm water hull clearance height.

Contouring – motion of a fixed foil craft when following a wave profile.

Intermediate response over high waves of a craft with automatically-controlled fully-submerged foils.

*Left:* Water screw driven via an inclined shaft.

*Right:* Screw driven by a Vee-drive. Like the inclined shaft, this system is used in hydrofoils with keels only a limited height above the water level.

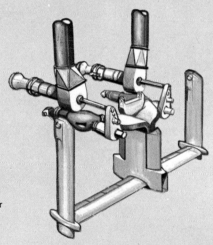

*Above:* The French-designed SOGREAH water pump propulsion system.

*Above:* Waterjet propulsion system employed on the Boeing Jetfoil. The two axial-flow pumps each deliver 22,300 g.p.m. and a thrust of 18,000 lb (80,000N).

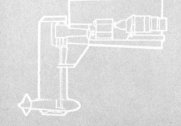

*Left:* Z-drive. Power is transmitted to the screw via a bevel gear over the stern, a vertical shaft, then via a second bevel gear to a horizontal propeller shaft. This arrangement provides a much greater clearance height than the Vee-drive or inclined shaft.

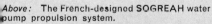

Vikhr, a 'coastal liner' carries 268 passengers on Black Sea routes.

Burevestnik, driven by gas-turbine driven waterjets.

Strela, a 94-seater operating on the Black Sea.

Kometa, one of Russia's most successful passenger hydrofoils, *below*.

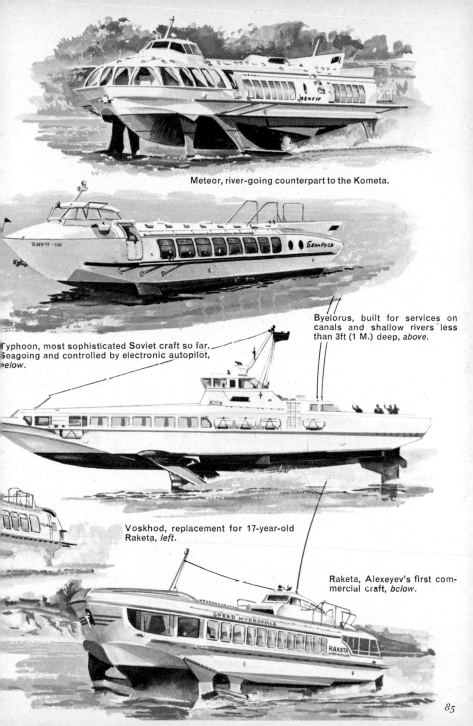

Meteor, river-going counterpart to the Kometa.

Byelorus, built for services on canals and shallow rivers less than 3ft (1 M.) deep, *above*.

Typhoon, most sophisticated Soviet craft so far. Seagoing and controlled by electronic autopilot, *below*.

Voskhod, replacement for 17-year-old Raketa, *left*.

Raketa, Alexeyev's first commercial craft, *below*.

## FIGHTING FOILCRAFT

The US Navy has played a dominant rôle in the development of the hydrofoils since the mid-1950s. It sees the hydrofoil as one of the best means of defence against fast missile craft, destroyers and submerged nuclear submarines, particularly when weather slows down all other craft except the submerged system hydrofoil.

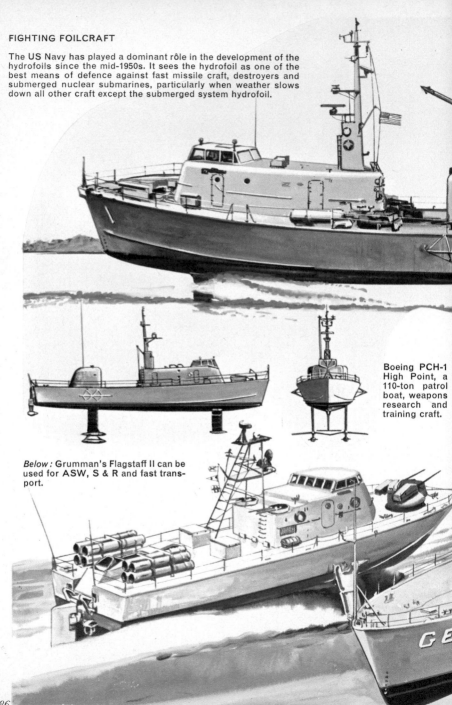

Boeing PCH-1 High Point, a 110-ton patrol boat, weapons research and training craft.

*Below:* Grumman's Flagstaff II can be used for ASW, S & R and fast transport.

*Right:* Boeing's Tucumcari hydro-foil gunboat which finally convinced Western navies of the advantages of the hydrofoil.

*Below:* World's biggest hydrofoil, the Grumman-designed AGEH-1 Plainview.

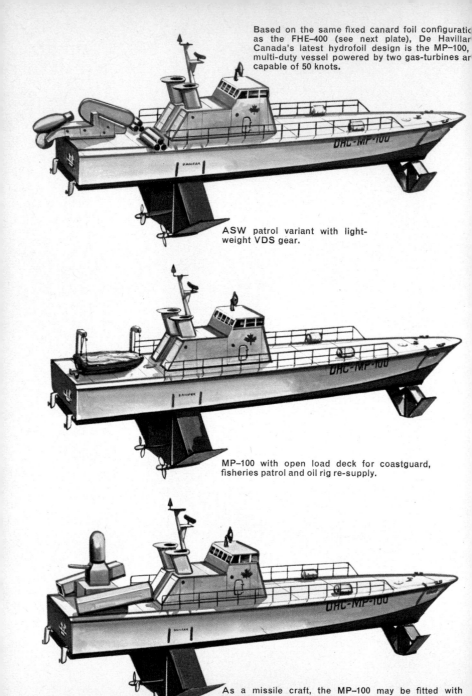

Based on the same fixed canard foil configuration as the FHE-400 (see next plate), De Havilland Canada's latest hydrofoil design is the MP-100, multi-duty vessel powered by two gas-turbines and capable of 50 knots.

ASW patrol variant with light-weight VDS gear.

MP-100 with open load deck for coastguard, fisheries patrol and oil rig re-supply.

As a missile craft, the MP-100 may be fitted with Harpoon or Exocet missiles. A Vulcan gun is mounted aft for self-defence.

One of the world's fastest hydrofoils is the Royal Canadian Navy's FHE-400, built to establish the feasibility of operating a hydrofoil escort vessel of 230 tons in ocean conditions. It has attained 63 knots in calm water and speeds in excess of 40 knots in 10—15 ft waves. A fresh series of trials is contemplated in which the vessel, commissioned as HMCS *Bras d'Or*, will be equipped for ASW duties.

# NATO'S MINI BATTLESHIP

230-ton waterjet-propelled Boeing hydrofoil, the PHM was designed in response to a NATO requirement for a fast patrol craft. The US Navy's version, *shown below,* will carry Harpoon anti-ship missiles
d a 76 mm Oto Melara dual purpose anti-aircraft, anti-ship cannon. PHMs, with a speed in excess of
knots, will operate from LSD (Landing Ships Dock) 'Mother ships' *left,* in addition to shore bases.

First missile-launching hydrofoil craft to be built for the Italian Navy is the 62.5 ton Swordfish, an improved version of the Boeing PGH-2 Tucumcari. The first of four of this class, named Sparviero, was delivered to the Italian Navy in the Spring of 1974. Powered by a 4,500 shp Rolls-Royce Proteus gas-turbine driving a waterjet, the vessel has a top speed of 50 knots in calm water. Armament comprises two fixed launchers for Otomat ship-to-ship missiles and a 76mm Oto Melara automatic anti-aircraft gun.

# CHAPTER ONE

# WORLD OF SKIMMERS

To skim the surface of the waters at the speed of the wind with the effortless grace of the gulls has been the dream of the seagoer since the dawn of time. But in spite of centuries of inventive effort, the ability to achieve this goal has totally evaded him until recently. Supersonic flight, the harnessing of nuclear energy and even the moon landings have all proved easier by far than the design of a vehicle capable of sustaining high speeds across the violently undulating face of the seas and oceans.

Over the years, shipowners have looked on helplessly as the speed of competitive forms of transport in other spheres has risen incessantly, while the speed of their own craft has dropped further and further behind. Little wonder then, that the shipping world has a long tradition of conservatism, and tends to be sceptical about new ship concepts. Seafarers still hold the belief that, if during the first 5,000 years of nautical history, no-one has designed a vessel to replace the displacement ship, how can any-one possibly hope to build such a vessel today?

In terms of performance how do conventional ships compare with other modes of transport? From the day they were first introduced, the speeds of trains, cars and commercial aircraft have increased tenfold. Since the inauguration of the Darlington-Stockton railway in 1825, when 10 mph was attained, rail speeds have risen to over 100 mph; the top speed of the first practical car was 12 mph, while that of today's vehicle is 120 mph. Faster still, airliner speeds have surged upwards from 60–75 mph to 600 mph—and when Concorde services begin they will be twenty times as fast. Against this, ship speeds have risen less than threefold since 1858 when the *Great Eastern*, the largest vessel of its time, attained 14.5 knots. Today, one of the fastest passenger ships, the *Queen Elizabeth II*, averages 30 knots—barely twice as fast. On Europe's lakes and rivers, the most modern displacement craft run at only twice the speed of their predecessors of 100 years ago.

What makes this lack of progress all the more perplexing is that in almost every other field of human endeavour, the past 100 years have proved, in the technological sense, the most amazingly fruitful period since the birth of Man.

Down the ages, the two main problems besetting the ship designer in his quest for higher performance have remained unchanged—the nature and density of the very medium through which the ship travels, and its ever-changing contours. Since water is 815 times denser than air, resistance to a ship's passage is immensely greater than that encountered by land vehicles or aircraft. Another difficulty is that the water resistance, or drag, increases geometrically in relation to the speed of the ship, which means that very considerable increases in engine power are required for relatively small improvements in performance. A final hurdle—the higher the speed attained by a displacement craft in waves, the greater is the discomfort experienced by its occupants and the more the likelihood of damage being incurred to the vessel and its cargo.

At first, naval architects were convinced that the overall shape of the conventional hull could not be improved, and that the only way to overcome water resistance was to reduce the volume of the craft normally immersed. The first major move towards improved performance was the construction of a number of craft with flat and shallow V-shaped bottoms, in which dynamic lifting forces took over as the vessels gathered speed, thus raising much of the hull out of the water. Many of the designs failed because they were unable to achieve the speeds required. Those that did were extremely unpleasant to travel in when operating in waves, as vertical accelerations of 6 g and more were encountered by the occupants. While this intense discomfort could be endured for short periods by crews of naval vessels and racing craft, it was by no means acceptable to fare-paying passengers in commercial craft. Yet another drawback soon became apparent. At high speeds on rivers the V-hulled craft created a strong wake which not only interfered with the safe operation of other craft, but also seriously eroded river banks.

Between the 1850's and 1900, several far-sighted inventors realised that in order to provide both speed and comfort, it was necessary to evolve a system capable firstly of lifting the hull bodily free of the water, and secondly of 'uncoupling' it from the continual motion of the waves. Their solutions marked the origins of two new classes of marine vehicles—air-cushion vehicles and hydrofoils.

Both were designed to overcome water drag, and to a large

extent the effects of wave motion, by raising their hulls above the surface—one by lifting itself out of the water on either a static or dynamic cushion of air, the other by using the hydrodynamic lift created by the forward motion of underwater foils or wings. Both concepts are regarded as having the development potential for increasing overwater speeds to at least 100 knots, and in the case of large vehicles, riding like low-flying aircraft on a dynamic cushion of air, this speed can be more than doubled.

Over the past two decades, increasing encouragement and financial backing from both private and government sources has led to the construction of many examples of both types of vessel. Growing numbers of small air-cushion vehicles and hydrofoils are in service today on inland and coastal waters the world over. Few of these craft weigh more than 200 tons, and not many have been designed to venture out into open seas. But now most of the problems have been mastered, very much bigger vessels are under development for use, not only on the open seas, but also for inter-continental services.

During the past fifteen years, surface skimming craft have succeeded in doubling or even trebling over-water speeds, and have brought about one of the most dramatic changes in the history of seafaring. Within the next twenty years, travel by skimmers can be expected to become more commonplace than air travel.

## Riding on air

The earliest recorded attempt to design an air-cushion vehicle was that of Emmanuel Swedenborg, the Swedish designer and philosopher, who in 1716 proposed a vehicle rather like an upturned dinghy with a cockpit in the centre. Apertures on either side of this allowed the operator to raise and lower a pair of oar-like air scoops, which on the downward strokes would force compressed air beneath the hull, thus raising it above the surface. The project was short-lived, for Swedenborg soon realised that to operate such a machine required a source of energy far greater than that which could be supplied by a single human occupant.

Much of the early development work was concentrated on the reduction of hydrodynamic drag by lubricating the base of the hull with a thin layer of compressed air, for it had been discovered that pressurised air reacted against the water surface, causing the vessel to skim over it rather than through it. Proposals for this approach date back to the 1860's. The records of the British Patent Office indicate that Lord Thornycroft started experiments with air-lubricated hulls in 1874 and by 1875 correspondence on possible applications was being exchanged between Admiralty constructors in the United Kingdom and the Netherlands. The next twenty-five years saw hundreds of British, American and Swedish inventors hard at work on this approach, but none appear to have succeeded in producing a working example. However, in the United States in 1897, a Mr Cuthbertson filed a patent in which, with surprising accuracy, he forecast the configuration of today's sidewall air-cushion vehicle. His patent described the lift system thus: 'Air compressors force air through compartments so the water has small frictional engagement with the hull. It [the air] will pass to the stern and present a cushion intervening [between] the hull and the water.'

In 1909, a Swedish engineer, Hans Dineson, completed the detailed design of a sidewall ACV featuring flexible rubber cushion seals fore and aft, and in 1916, Dagobert Muller von Thomamhul, an Austrian engineer, designed and built a sidewall ACV torpedo-boat for the Austrian navy. Details are scarce, but drawings and at least one photograph exist. According to reports of the time, it attained a speed of 40 knots, and as far as is known, this was the world's first successful air-cushion vehicle. Further development was evidently abandoned after the catastrophe which overtook the Austro-Hungarian Empire as a result of World War I.

Over the ensuing forty years, sporadic efforts were made by a score or more of inventors to interest private backers and governments, but they seldom attracted more than momentary interest, and as their funds ran out, so their projects were either shelved or died. Nevertheless, at least three of these pioneer 'hovernauts' managed to make some impact on the news media of their day. They were A. V. Alcock, an Australian who built a series of successful working models during the period 1912–39, and who coined the term 'floating traction' for this kind of transport; Douglas Kent Warner, who entered one of his early sidewall sports craft in the Middleton races on the Connecticut river in 1930, and T. J. Kaario of Finland. Tovio Kaario, who is still conducting ACV experiments today, attained a speed of 12 knots over ice with his first ram-wing single-seater in 1935 while employed by the Valmet Aircraft Company. But it was not until

Christopher Cockerell's achievements were reported by the world's press in 1959 that international recognition was given to the potential of this form of transportation.

Cockerell, like most of the earlier pioneers, began by exploring the use of air lubrication to reduce hydrodynamic drag, employing first a punt, then a 20-knot ex-Naval launch as testcraft. The limitation of this approach quickly became apparent, and before long he was fired with a far more ambitious idea, one in which the thin layer of lubricating air gave way to a deep air-cushion which would raise the craft above the surface, enabling it not only to clear small waves, but also to make the transition from water to land and back again. The result of his famed experiments with an industrial blower unit and coffee tins was the hovercraft principle. Unlike earlier plenum-type air-cushion vehicles, in which air was simply forced by a fan into a larger chamber beneath the vehicle and allowed to escape, Cockerell's system employed a jet of air expelled from the outer periphery of the base of the craft with the 'nozzle' aimed downwards and inwards to form a continuous air curtain. This minimised air leakage and provided a much greater ground clearance than the earlier machines for the lift power expended.

The first full-scale craft to employ the principle was the Government-backed Saunders-Roe SR.N1, which in the early hours of 25 July 1959—the fiftieth anniversary of Bleriot's epic English Channel flight—successfully skimmed over the same route, from Calais to Dover, setting down on the beach by Dover Clock Tower before most people had risen for work that day. To those who were out and about, the sight of the cotton-reel-like craft wafting across the harbour and up the beach was a page from science fiction come to life. Watching it manoeuvre to-and-fro on the sand below, they could scarcely have imagined that within little more than a decade its descendants, giants fifty times its weight and three times as fast, would carry annually one third of all the passengers and car traffic across the same waters.

News of the crossing stirred the imagination of those involved in waterborne transportation throughout the world. At first it seemed as if the peripheral jet would provide sufficient clearance height to allow a medium-size craft to negotiate coastal waters, at least, without employing more than one-half or one-quarter of the power required by a conventional aeroplane or helicopter of similar capacity. But in practice, the clearance height was only one-twentieth or one-thirtieth of its beam. This meant that craft

40 ft wide and 80 ft long would have a clearance between the base of their hardstructure and the surface beneath of only 1–2 ft. Had this situation continued, the air-cushion vehicle would not have advanced beyond the stage of an interesting aerodynamic phenomenon, with very limited practical application apart from moving heavy machinery over flat hard surfaces.

But with remarkable foresight, another inventor, C. H. Latimer-Needham, had anticipated just such a problem. Early in 1958, after reading that Christopher Cockerell was experimenting with a new form of air-cushion locomotion, he thought of the size of the waves that these craft would encounter in the English Channel and the Atlantic and was convinced that obstacles of this sort clearly called for a form of flexible skirt to contain the air cushion and enable the vessels to traverse significantly rougher surfaces. On contact with the obstacle, the skirt would tend to collapse, but by reducing the peripheral diameter at the base, either by built-in taper or curvature, there would be a downward component of force tending to keep the skirt extended.

In October 1961, Latimer-Needham sold his skirt patents to Westland, the parent company of Saunders-Roe Ltd, which built the SR.N1. The earliest Westland skirts were simply extensions of the inner and outer edges of the peripheral air ducts at the base of the hardstructure, made in two sheets of rubberised fabric and feeding air into the cushion through the gap that separated the two skirts at the hemline. Air from the lift fan simply entered between the two walls of the skirt, which then inflated, and was discharged into the cushion at its base. As the skirt concept was developed, so easily replaceable 'fingers' or loops of material were fastened at the hemline to reduce water drag and take the wear.

The introduction of the skirt was a vital engineering breakthrough, just as important in its way as the invention of the pneumatic tyre and a car's suspension system. It meant that the total depth of the air-cushion beneath the solid structure was now equal to the depth of the skirt, plus the daylight clearance or hovergap between the skirt hemline and the ground. Excited engineers at Westland soon ascertained that, for a given power, the obstacle clearance height was ten times greater. Apart from being subjected to very considerable wear and tear, particularly at high speed over water, it was felt that it would offer few operational problems. It would deflect on coming into contact

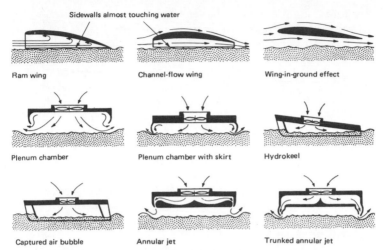

Ram wing

Channel-flow wing

Wing-in-ground effect

Plenum chamber

Plenum chamber with skirt

Hydrokeel

Captured air bubble

Annular jet

Trunked annular jet

*Air-cushion vehicles are divided into two different categories, those supported by a self-generated cushion of air and those dependent upon forward speed to develop lift, like an aeroplane. Those in the first category are known as aerostatic types, and those in the latter, aerodynamic. In aerostatic craft, the cushion is put down under pressure by a fan or fans and contained beneath the hull by flexible skirts or seals or by rigid sidewalls.*

with waves, rocks and jetties, and since afterwards it would return promptly to its normal inflated shape, air leakage would be minimal.

Just how effective the skirt was destined to become was dramatically demonstrated on the SR.N1. In 1959 the skirtless craft could only operate in calm seas and negotiate 6–9 in obstacles. By mid-1962, with 4-ft deep skirts fitted, a spectacular transformation had taken place. It could now operate at 50 knots over a relatively smooth surface, at 40 knots in 4/5-ft seas, and at reduced speed, it could cope with 6/7-ft waves. Marshland with gullies up to 4-ft deep could be traversed and it could safely cross outcrops up to 3 ft 6 in. high. Moreover, the craft was now operating at twice its original weight with no increase in lift power.

Westland had now been joined in hovercraft manufacture in the United Kingdom by Vickers, Britten-Norman, Folland Aircraft and Denny (the ACV interests of the former two were later to be taken over by British Hovercraft Corporation, a Westland subsidiary), by Bell, Ford, Republic Aviation, General

Dynamics, and several smaller companies in the USA; by Mitsui and Mitsubishi in Japan; Bertin in France; Saab in Sweden and Sormovo and the Leningrad Admiralty Shipyards in the Soviet Union.

During the late 1950's and early 1960's, a number of inventors in the United States had also been active in the air-cushion vehicle field, and some were nearly abreast of Cockerell. One, Colonel Melville Beardsley, filed patents covering a similar peripheral jet system only a matter of twelve weeks after Christopher Cockerell had filed his. Many other Americans, including Dr William R. Bertelsen, Tom Sweeney, Harvey Chaplin, Walter A. Crowley and Douglas Warner were all engaged in testing man-carrying ground-effect machines (GEMs) as they were then known. The relatively slow progress made in the United States at this time has been put down to the lack of government interest and only minimal industrial effort.

ACV pioneers were active in other countries too. In Brazil in August 1955, a few months *before* Christopher Cockerell received his first patent, Renalto Alves De Lima filed a provisional application for a patent covering vehicles using a similar jet curtain concept which, he predicted, could also be used on aircraft in place of a conventional landing gear

Another fascinating approach was that of Carl Weiland, a young Swiss, who worked with the Federal Aircraft Organisation before leaving for the United States. Weiland's first craft reached 60 mph during trials on Lake Zürich. Air for the cushion was compressed in annular compartments separated by a skeg or labyrinth and as it escaped from the first compartment it was drawn up by a fan into the next one and then forced back. This was known as the recirculation system.

Before long, plans for operating these vessels for profit, pleasure and public service were being pursued on nearly every continent. Within a decade, a variety of commercial and military hovercraft of between 6 and 50 tons were in service throughout the world. The best known are BHC's SR.N4, N5, N6 and BH.7, the Cushion Craft CC-7, Hovermarine's HM.2, Mitsui's MV-PP.5, Sedam's N.300, Bell's Voyageur and Viking, and Sormovo's Sormovich and Zarnitsa. The biggest is British Hovercraft Corporation's 200-ton SR.N4 Mountbatten-class, passenger/car ferry, the first of which entered service with British Rail Hovercraft Ltd on its English Channel Dover–Boulogne service in 1968. Since then it has been joined on the Channel by four others, three of them operated by Hoverlloyd Ltd on the Ramsgate–Calais service. Between them they carry upwards of 1.4 million passengers and 200,000 cars annually, representing nearly 30 per cent. of all the passenger and car traffic ferried across these turbulent waters. Cross-channel, island-to-island and mainland-to-island links employing air-cushion vehicles are now in the minds of operating companies the world over.

In the Arctic regions of Canada, Alaska and the Soviet Union, air-cushion vehicles are seen as the only practical means of opening up these areas, which are covered by ice in winter and by spongy, boggy tundra in summer. Vehicles of modular construction, like the Voyageur and Viking, are designed to be dismantled and flown into their operating areas in the far north aboard large transport aircraft. Once assembled, they act as feeders from the Arctic airstrips carrying containers, equipment, supplies and passengers to exploration and mining sites and other communities.

In Russia, tens of thousands of miles of lakes, rivers and seas freeze-up during the winter, leaving displacement vessels and hydrofoils inoperable until the following spring. Skirted and aerodynamic ACVs have the advantage of being able to maintain year-round services, as well as being the only fast craft capable of operating on the many shallow rivers in the Soviet Far East during the summer navigation season, where, for long stretches, the water is only a few feet deep.

As early as 1950, awareness was growing as to the potential of the air-cushion vehicle as a military vehicle. It was soon realised that substantial cost benefits could stem from the replacement of conventional warships—large patrol boats, frigates, assault landing craft, ASW (anti-submarine warfare) vessels and others —by fast, compact craft that overcame the water speed barrier and completed a given task in a third of the time or less than that required previously. Additional attractions were the degree of automation that could be used, leading to a reduction in the number of crew members and the multi-terrain capability of all but the solid sidewall craft. Because of the shallow floating draft of the skirted types, it was no longer necessary to depend on deep-water ports and anchorages, which for a century or more had been considered a prerequisite of a strong sea defence system.

The vessels could be equipped with the same lightweight ship-to-ship and ship-to-air missiles which were about to be installed on conventional warships, and this meant that a small,

75-ton ACV could challenge a conventional 2,000–3,000-ton warship on more than equal terms, since the displacement destroyer or frigate would have the dual disadvantage of being a very much bigger target and far slower than its high-speed, hard-hitting adversary.

The beginning of the new generation of military vehicles was marked by the dispatch of three 7-ton Bell SK-5s by the US Navy to Vietnam in 1966. These were converted, BHC-built SR.N5s, and except for their power plant, armour and guns were identical to the commercial model. In 1968 they were joined by three US Army SK.5s, which were built by Bell at Buffalo, New York, and were more heavily armed and armoured than their predecessors. The six vehicles, which were employed on patrol and search and rescue operations, logged more than 10,000 hours during the Vietnam war.

The next step was the development of the much larger and more powerful JEFF(A) and (B) 150-ton Amphibious Assault Landing Craft by Aerojet-General and Bell for the US Navy and Marine Corps. But more spectacular by far is the plan of the US Navy's Surface Effect Ship Project Office to build a prototype, 2,200-ton surface effect ship* by mid-1981. The first stage was the construction of two 1/20th scale 100-ton manned testcraft, the Aerojet-General SES-100A and the Bell Aerospace SES-100B— both of which have proved capable of speeds of 70 knots or more in 2-ft waves. Waterjet propulsion is employed on the Aerojet-General craft, and partially-submerged, super-cavitating pro- pellers used on the Bell design, which has been tested in the Gulf of Mexico in wave heights in excess of 8 ft.

The projected vessel, designated 2KSES, will be eleven times the displacement of the 200-ton SR.N4, the biggest hovercraft operating today, and of approximately the same size as a small World War II destroyer. The US Navy believes that a 2,200-ton SES is the smallest size craft suitable for testing on the open ocean and until a vessel of this size is available, it will be difficult to determine the feasibility of even bigger SESs.

If the 2,200-ton prototype proves effective, the US Navy plans to introduce an operational class of 2,000–3,000-ton SESs for use as escorts, small helicopter and V/STOL aircraft platforms and

---

* *US Navy term for a ship-size, seagoing air-cushion vehicle or hovercraft employing rigid sidewalls integral to the hull structure and flexible seals fore and aft to contain the air cushion.*

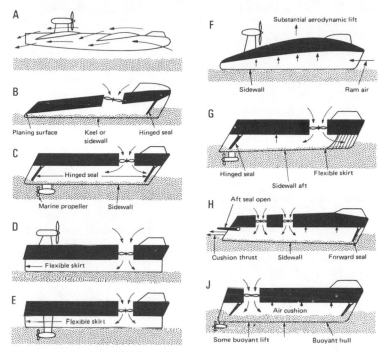

*Surface Effect Ship (SES) configurations: A. Wing-in-ground-effect (also known as Aerofoil Boat or Ekranoplan types); B. Air-lubricated hull or hydro-keel; C. Sidewall SES (may be propelled by waterjets); D. Air-propelled amphibious SES; E. Water-screw propelled, semi-amphibious SES; F. Ram-wing SES; G. Hybrid SES with rigid sidewalls and bow skirts (like C, may be propelled by waterjets); H. Airjet SES propelled by air bled from cushion fans; J. Aircat SES with wide buoyant hulls. (With acknowledgements to E. K. Liberatore, Aeromar Corporation.)*

missile-armed surface combatants. At the same time, it is examining concepts for craft of 6–10,000 tons. During the fighting in Jordan in 1970, it took eleven days to move a battalion of US Marines 5,600 miles to the Eastern Mediterranean to reinforce the 6th Fleet. Surface effect ships, according to one US Admiral, could have completed the task in seventy-two hours. They will each be capable of fulfilling several different roles including anti-submarine warfare, amphibious assault, early warning, aircraft strikes and logistic supply. In troop carrier configuration, they are seen as a possible means of economising in defence expenditure, by allowing more troops to be retained in US bases instead of overseas.

Another US Navy project is for a 600-ton vehicle to demonstrate the potential of the skirted SES as a long-range military platform to service military bases and early warning systems in the Arctic. It will be the only vehicle capable of roaming the ridged wastes of pack ice under all weather and temperature conditions on a 24-hour basis. A vessel capable of making the transition from sea to ice, traversing Arctic wastes without reducing speed, then skimming out across another ocean could well revolutionise marine surface transportation concepts.

The SES's military potential has been summed up by Dr Robert A. Frosch, Assistant Secretary for the US Navy, who stated that it is likely to 'change the whole nature of surface naval warfare as it will lead to ships that can move at speeds and with capabilities that have never been seen before on the surface of the ocean'.

But the future of the SES is by no means limited to military applications. For example, the development of large vessels for the Arctic may well result in the wide commercial employment of similar vehicles within and across this zone. As transit vehicles, they would permit a very considerable reduction in the sea travel distance between the North Atlantic and the North Pacific. On some routes, such as London–Tokyo and London–Anchorage, the reduction in distance would be as much as 40 per cent. Because of their high speed, the transit time would be only about 1/10th that of a displacement vessel. Vehicles used for commercial operations would be employed for moving people and cargo across the ice-cap between Arctic and northern terrain, as well as to bases in the south. Major roles would be the support of oil and mineral extraction and the trans-shipment of food and furs, construction materials and machinery.

The skimmer industry today caters not only for defence and commercial operators, but also for the enthusiast. Small sporting machines of one or two seats are becoming increasingly popular and craft with up to six seats are now being produced and marketed for personnel and light freight transport, surveying and various other utility applications. Rallies are held frequently for the smaller craft and often attract between 20–30 entrants.

Another area of increasing activity is the industrial field, where more and more companies are employing hovertrailers and large hoverplatforms to traverse marshy or ice-bound terrain. A variety of heavy lift systems are in use the world over to lay pipelines, undertake oil surveys, and conduct land reclamation and irrigation schemes in areas in which it is impossible to drive wheeled or tracked vehicles under load. A direct descendant of Hovercraft Development Ltd's air-cushion vehicle skirt system is the industrial skirt, which is now being employed throughout the world to move a wide variety of heavy loads, one of the biggest of which was a 700-ton storage tank. The equipment consists simply of a wrap-around segmented skirt, one or more engine/fan units and air hosing to convey pressurised air to the skirt. It can be shipped or airfreighted easily to sites anywhere and is proving a boon to the oil industry. Once on its air cushion, the load is either winched or towed to its new location.

The rate of advance of the hovercraft from laboratory experiment to operational status has been quicker than that of any other form of vehicle. The diversity of roles that the ACV and its load-carrying offshoots are called upon to fulfil continues to increase. Many of its applications are described and illustrated in the chapters that follow, but undoubtedly there will be many other even more exciting roles for it to play in future.

# Flight on foils

The hydrofoil represents a marriage of the high-speed boat to the aeroplane. It has been described as 'a blend of aerodynamics and hydrodynamics—a cross between the ship which it looks like and an aeroplane which it is built like'.

It can hardly come as a surprise then to find that many pioneers in aviation—Forlanini, the Wright brothers, Comte de Lambert, Clement Ader, Alexander Graham Bell, Glenn Curtiss, 'Casey' Baldwin and Lieutenant Selfridge among them—were also to the forefront in the pioneering days of hydrofoils. In fact, the link between individuals and companies in aviation and hydrofoil design has persisted to such a degree that it is almost a tradition. One has only to list some of the major aerospace companies active in this field in recent times—Boeing, De Havilland Canada, Grumman, Lockheed, Aérospatiale, Blohm & Voss, Hitachi and Mitsubishi—to define the extent of the aviation connection. If we add to these the names of the leading hydrofoil powerplant manufacturers—Allison, Aerojet-General, General Electric, Pratt & Whitney, Rolls-Royce, MTU and Turbomeca—it becomes clear that with two or three notable exceptions, it is the aerospace rather than the shipbuilding industry which has taken up the challenge and provided the momentum for hydrofoil development.

Unlike the air-cushion vehicle, which is raised above the water or other supporting surface by either a static or dynamic cushion of pressurised air, the hydrofoil is raised bodily above the water surface by small wing-like foils, similar in section to the wings of an aircraft, and designed to generate lift.

Although the foil moves through water, which is 815 times the density of air, it operates on the identical principle to that of an aerofoil. Dr Daniel Bernoulli, in his study of gases and fluids in motion, showed that the faster a fluid or gas moves, the lower the pressure it exerts upon objects along which it flows. In exactly the same way as an aerofoil, the curved upper surface of the hydrofoil causes water to flow at higher speeds above it than beneath it, causing a difference of pressure between upper and lower surfaces. The water streaming over the curved upper surface has to move faster than that flowing beneath, leading to a reduction of pressure on the upper surface and increased pressure on the lower surface. The foils are connected to the hull by struts and at a given speed the lift generated by the foils raises the hull bodily out of the water.

The first successful hydrofoil was one of a series of 'Hydro-Aeroplanes' designed and built by the Italian helicopter and airship pioneer, Enrico Forlanini. His craft was equipped with foils set like the rungs of a ladder. It was demonstrated on a number of occasions on Lake Maggiore during 1905–11, and could attain 38 knots. In 1907 Forlanini was joined on Lake Maggiore by another aviator, General Arturo Crocco, who built the first-ever hydrofoil boat to possess a dihedral surface-piercing foil system, generally known as a vee-foil configuration. Crocco tried hard to market the advantages of the hydrofoil and mailed pamphlets extolling its merits as a high-speed runabout for inland waterways, but with no avail. Many years later, however, his foils inspired the Schertel–Sachsenburg system, which was eventually used on the first hydrofoil boats in the world to enter commercial service.

Although Forlanini and Crocco were the first to build full-size craft which operated under their own power, the first known experiments with foil configurations had been undertaken between ten and twenty years earlier. In the United Kingdom in 1881, Horatio Phillips conceived the first ladder foil system which was successfully demonstrated with the aid of towed models, and in 1894, two brothers, M. and L. Meacham designed a boat equipped with fully submerged incidence-controlled foils. A planing sensor, attached to a feeler arm aft of the forward foils, was designed to vary their angle of incidence and hence lift, according to the height of the waves, but there is no record of the craft being built.

Another frequently mentioned pioneer is Comte de Lambert, who demonstrated a craft on the Seine in 1891. Although his boat has been described many times as a hydrofoil, it was in fact a planing craft with foils at the sides intended for high-speed skimming rather than foiling. De Lambert gave up his high-speed boat experiments without ever having built a true hydrofoil and later became involved in French aviation.

In 1911, Forlanini found his first hydrofoil client. After a ride in one of his Hydro-Aeroplanes on Lake Maggiore, Alexander Graham Bell, inventor of the telephone, became so enthused with the concept, that he purchased a licence to build and develop the Forlanini ladder-foil system in North America. Among Bell's associates in this venture were 'Casey' Baldwin, Glenn Curtiss, Lieutenant Selfridge and John McCurdy. Bell incidentally called his craft Hydrodromes, and one of these, the HD-4, set up a world waterspeed record of 70.86 mph in September 1918.

Forlanini was the first inventor to export a hydrofoil design, but it was Bell's associate, 'Casey' Baldwin, who exported the first finished craft. Two of Bell's Hydrodromes were supplied to the Royal Navy in the early 1920's. Soon after their delivery, they were put through high-speed towing tests off Spithead in a heavy gale. Their structures were not designed to withstand the sea state and the two craft fell apart.

Due, probably, to the non-availability of suitable lightweight marine powerplants, an almost total lack of experience in the construction of lightweight metal boat structures and absence of government support, interest in hydrofoils appears to have waned until 1927, when Baron Hanns von Schertel, founder of Supramar Ltd, began his experiments in Germany.

Like Forlanini, von Schertel was also an engineer and an aviation enthusiast. In 1924 he entered the Rhoen Sailplane competition and was presented with a prize for designing a sailplane with a variable-lift wing section. It was not until 1936, however, after he had built his eighth experimental hydrofoil, that he could claim to have defeated the ventilation, foil design and propulsion problems that plagued all earlier designs and to have built an inherently stable boat capable of operating foil-borne in waves in complete safety.

Von Schertel, now acknowledged as the father of the modern hydrofoil, celebrated his success with a 230-mile (370-km) flight from Mainz to Cologne and back in bad weather, a feat which so convinced the board of the Köln–Düsseldorfer Shipping Line, the Rhine ferry operators, of the future of the concept that they promptly placed an order for the first passenger hydrofoil boat. The order led to the formation, in association with the late Herr Sachsenburg, of the Schertel–Sachsenburg Hydrofoil Consortium, its first licensee being the Gebrüder Sachsenburg Shipyard. The aim of the Consortium was to exploit the patents and technical achievements of Hanns von Schertel and to facilitate the development of his design with the co-operation of the shipyard. The yard was under the technical management of Professor G. Weinblum and possessed a team of very highly qualified engineers. From then on all design and construction was accompanied by large-scale theoretical and experimental research, and model tests.

In 1939, just before the outbreak of World War II, the Consortium completed a 2.8-ton demonstration craft, which immediately aroused the interest of the German Navy. After a demonstration in the Baltic, craft were ordered by both the German Navy and the Army. The military requirements took priority, and because of the intervention of the war and the upheavals in its wake, it was another fourteen years before Hanns von Schertel was able to launch his first commercial hydrofoil.

Work on the first naval vessel, the 17-ton VS.6, started in June 1940. The object was to run competitive trials between a hydrofoil minelayer and a conventional displacement minelayer of similar dimensions, weight and engine output. Tests were held the following year, when the VS.6 attained 47.5 knots—some 17.5 knots faster than the conventional minelayer. This was an astonishing achievement, especially when seen in retrospect, for it was another twenty-five years before this speed could be matched by another hydrofoil vessel—the US Maritime Administration's Grumman Denison.

Fifteen different hydrofoil boats of various sizes were developed during the war, the largest being a 105-ft long, 80-ton long-range fast cargo craft, capable of carrying a 20-ton Army tank, ammunition and supplies between Sicily and North Africa. A maximum speed of 40 knots was obtained using a pair of 3,600-hp Mercedes-Benz diesels. This particular craft was left stranded in 1944 after both engines failed in a storm. During trials under full load it had proved to be capable of operating at 37 knots in waves up to 6 ft high and 150 ft in length.

During his wartime association with the extremely competent design team under Dr Weinblum at Gebrüder Sachsenburg, von Schertel had been able to undertake exhaustive studies of cavitation, supercavitation, ventilation and other phenomena, and by 1945 he had found solutions to most of the problems which had beset hydrofoil design since the earliest days.

To overcome the sea-clearance limitations of inclined and vee-drives, Schertel had even built the first hydrofoil Z-drive system. His T 1–6 coastal surveillance craft had an engine in the stern which was connected to a pair of contra-rotating propellers by a double-bevel gear designed at the Sachsenburg yard. This craft, together with the work that he and his team had undertaken at Dessau–Rosslau was taken over by the Soviet Union immediately after the occupation of Eastern Germany, together with a number of other finished and half-assembled experimental craft, one of which could attain 60 knots. Work continued at this yard for some years before it was decided to concentrate all hydrofoil design and construction activity within the Eastern bloc at the Leningrad Marine Institute, Leningrad Admiralty Shipyards and the Sormovo Shipyard at Gorki.

Senior engineers at MTU, the West German diesel engine and gas-turbine manufacturer, recall that their first experience in hydrofoil diesel engine propulsion was in Dessau–Rosslau in 1948, when the company was approached to assist in the development of the Soviet Navy's TK-class torpedo-boat under construction at the former Sachsenburg Yard. The boat was designed and constructed by the few remaining members of von Schertel's team. It was described by the Soviet occupation authorities as a fast passenger ferry and carried a small dummy passenger saloon superstructure as camouflage. Twin 2,500 hp Mercedes-Benz MB 511 diesels were fitted and before being driven to a Soviet port during the early stages of its trials, it achieved 47 knots. Several other craft were built in later years for the Soviet Navy, one of which had air-propulsion and fully-submerged foils. None remained long enough at the yard for the design team to reap much in the way of performance data. Trials were invariably interrupted after the second or third test and the craft was then whisked away to the Soviet Union.

The British Admiralty also took an interest in von Schertel's wartime activities and as soon as the naval base at Travenenmünde was occupied, the VS.6 was sequestered and brought to the British Isles. It was then tested and put into storage at *HMS Hornet*, one of the Royal Navy's land bases.

Eventually, Hanns von Schertel and several members of his Sachsenburg team were able to set up in business again at Lucerne, in Switzerland, under the name Supramar AG. Supramar's first post-war design was the 28-passenger PT 10 (P—Passenger; T—Transport; 10—the original design weight in metric tonnes), a 9.2-ton fast ferry introduced into service on a route between Locarno and Arona on Lake Maggiore on 16th May 1953.

There was little in the way of strong competition on the route, the steamers were slow, and the coaches and trains were hampered by the mountainous nature of the terrain which meant time lost in negotiating deep bends. The steamer took 2 hours 50 minutes to cover the 33 nautical miles, and cars going around the lake took 1½ hours. The PT 10, foiling at 38 knots from pier to pier took 48 minutes, offering tourists what was far and away the quickest link between Italy and Switzerland at that point and business prospered. In fact, the craft was repeatedly run by its Swiss and Italian charterers with 50 per cent. more passengers than it was designed to carry, but with no appreciable reduction in performance.

Unlike the massive and enthusiastic response by the world's news media to the very marginal Channel crossing performed by the first hovercraft six years later, the enormous technical breakthrough represented by the PT 10 was completely overlooked. Happily, it did not escape attention altogether. For one imaginative tourist who decided to take a ride on this ingenious craft in 1953 was Carlo Rodriquez, head of the Cantiere Navale Rodriquez Shipyard at Messina, Sicily.

Rodriquez, who is dedicated to the cause of developing commerce and industry in Sicily, felt that fast, comfortable, passenger hydrofoils were the perfect craft to encourage tourists to make the sea trip to Sicily from the Italian mainland. Tourism and commerce would prosper, and if he built hydrofoils for export, it would aid the island in the industrial sense. Rodriquez became Supramar's first licensee and this ensured that, along with its other more classic claims to fame, Sicily would also become renowned as the birthplace of the modern commercial hydrofoil. The combination of Rodriquez' unbounded enthusiasm—also that of his two nephews—plus the unmatched expertise of the Supramar team proved unbeatable. Soon the hydrofoil was riding high as it never had before in purely peacetime conditions. The technology was proven—but another challenge was still to be faced. Could the hydrofoil make a profit in the face of strong competition? After half-a-century of development, the concept of the boat on wings had reached the point of no return.

The first Rodriquez-built vessel was the PT 20 prototype, designed to specifications laid down by Registro Italiano Navale and Germanische Lloyd. The craft, Freccia del Sole, with seats for seventy-five passengers and displacing 27 tons was launched in 1956. By the middle of the year she had completed several demonstration runs along the Italian coast and a round trip of 1,600 nautical miles from Italy to Greece. Her seaworthiness had been proved on many occasions and she had operated in waves up to 13 ft high.

In August 1956 Carlo Rodriquez started a shipping company called Aliscafi which was to specialise in operating these craft, not only in Italy, but anywhere else in the world where the hydrofoil could spread its sea wings. The company's first scheduled service was inaugurated in that same month between Sicily and the Italian mainland. The port-to-port time from Messina to Reggio di Calabria was cut down to one quarter of the time taken by the conventional ferry, and the craft made twenty-two trips daily, thus setting an example for the operation of other hydrofoil services.

Only four years later, von Schertel, addressing an American conference, was able to report: 'The results of this service are noteworthy. With a seating capacity of seventy-five passengers, one boat alone has carried a record number of 31,000 passengers in a single month. The average daily number of passengers is between 800–900. To date the boat has carried a total of 1,000,000 passengers. The boats operating around Sicily have covered a combined distance of approximately 465,000 nautical miles, which is more than the distance between the earth and the moon and back again.'

The hydrofoil had finally proved itself. It was commercially viable. By 1960, the PT 20 had been joined by the larger 63-ton

PT 50 and both were in full production. The PT 50 had almost twice the seating capacity of the PT 20 and was intended for use in open waters, further away from the coast, including inter-island services. The prototype was completed in early 1958 by the Rodriquez shipyard, and the design was soon approved by almost every marine classification society.

Before long the demand for Supramar hydrofoils was such that additional licences for building the company's designs were issued to shipyards in the Netherlands, Norway and Japan. Within a few years, the hydrofoil had more than made up for its earlier lack of publicity. Newspapers, international magazines and television began charting its future and PT 20 number two—'Flying Fish'—was employed in the James Bond film 'Thunderball'. Oil companies began not only to attach their promotional insignia to the side of the craft but also to order them for oil rig support. Von Schertel's dream had been realised: the hydrofoil had not only been proven; more important still, it had been accepted and was here to stay.

In recent years, Supramar, now basically a design office, has moved on to larger craft, including the PT 75 and PT 150, the development of air stabilisation for improved passenger comfort, and fully-submerged foil systems for craft designed to operate in heavy sea states. These developments are illustrated and de-scribed in subsequent chapters.

Two more hydrofoil pioneers who were hard at work in the 1930's were Professor Otto Tietjens and Grunberg. In 1932, Tietjens evolved a method of improving the stability of surface-piercing, area-stabilised craft by placing the main foil just ahead of the centre of gravity, then sweeping it forward. The object was to provide a means of maintaining a bow-up trim whenever the craft experienced a sudden loss of lift. The main problem experienced with this approach was that the main foil had to be located almost in the centre of the craft, close to the centre of gravity, providing little to support the hull fore and aft. Proto-types were built for the German navy during World War II, but loading became a critical problem and development was dis-continued in favour of the Schertel–Sachsenburg design.

Grunberg (now W. A. Graig) patented his system in Paris in 1935. He approached the subject in complete ignorance of earlier efforts, and was therefore under no-one's influence and had no preconceived ideas. His objectives were to raise the hull above the water level by a wing or wings totally immersed in water, and to provide inherent longitudinal stability without the use of gadgetry. The principle of flight suggested the use of angle of attack variation. His system, which was later to be employed on Aquavion craft, the De Havilland Canada FHE-400, and certain Sormovo designs, comprises a stabiliser attached to the bow and behind this, a wing. The lift curve of the stabiliser, as the draught changes, is considerably more responsive than the corresponding wing curve. As operational conditions change— speed, weight and cg travel—so the wing sinks or rises relative to the stabiliser, thereby adjusting to demand the angle of attack. The stabiliser embodied in Grunberg's patent is a displacement float or a partly immersed hydrofoil, but hydroskis and planing subfoils can also be used, as in the case of the USSR's Sormovo shallow-draft submerged-foil types.

There are two basic foil systems; first the surface-piercing type, which is inherently stable, and secondly the fully-submerged type, which is not inherently stable. The depth of foil immersion has to be maintained by mechanical, electrical or other controlling devices. The surface-piercing system which is characterised by its natural stability, ease of construction, operational reliability and simplicity of maintenance, is ideal for inland waters, estuaries and coastal areas. However, for heavy sea conditions, the fully-submerged foil, though very much more complex, is superior because of its better performance in waves. Submerged foil craft have relatively small foils and the total weight of the vessel is above them. The vessel is therefore top heavy in just the same way as an inverted pendulum. If its attitude and height above the water were not monitored and controlled continually, it would capsize.

The world's first successful system for controlling fully-submerged foils was designed and built by an Englishman— Christopher Hook. Hook's interest in hydrofoils started in France in the late 1930's when he was impressed by the lift generated by some 4-ft sq. photographic plates which he was developing. Caught in France by the German occupation, he studied hydrodynamics and aeronautics in Vichy until 1942, when he escaped by ship to Portuguese S.E. Africa. From there he made his way to Kenya where he evoked the interest of Kenya and Uganda Railways, and was allowed to build his first craft—based on £20's worth of components salvaged from a Supermarine Walrus —in the railway workshops at Kisumu.

On his return to the UK he built a small two-seat demonstrator, the air-propelled 'Red Bug', which he displayed at the 1951 New York Boat Show. The success of the 'Red Bug' led to Hook designing a number of all-metal conversion kits employing outboard engines with long extensions, and a contract to build a hydrofoil amphibious landing craft for the US Navy. Hook's control system is a mechanical one, in which projecting or trailing wave sensors are employed to ride on the waves and continuously transmit their shape through a connecting linkage to vary the incidence of the main foils in order to maintain them at the required depth. His original runabout weighed half-a-ton or less, so it was a big jump in size to the US landing craft, which was to weigh 14 tons. Also the requirement was a particularly complex one: the craft had to be able to fly at full speed from the moment of launching right on to the beach and to retract its legs, including the power strut, while at full speed.

Halobates, as the craft was named, had no difficulty in meeting the US Navy's performance requirements. It impressed all as it flew through 6-ft waves with ease at a speed of 39 knots, but, ironically, the very system that enabled it to outfly all other entrants in this US Navy competition, was also its downfall. The long feeler arms so vital for sensing wave height were considered too clumsy and too vulnerable for a landing craft.

Later, Hook was able to suggest another, more compact arrangement, but by then, the purely mechanical sensor system was out of favour. The US Navy and Aerospace industry had adopted Hook's incidence-controlled foils but the function of the feeler arms was to be undertaken by electronic sensors. Hook's achievement was a major step forward. He had proved for the very first time that fully-submerged foils with a suitable sensor system worked, and that craft of relatively low tonnage, so equipped, could operate safely in virtually any wave direction, formation and height. The impact of his work cannot be over-estimated, for the performance of his variable-incidence controlled craft—built mainly under adverse conditions and on shoe-string budgets—helped silence some of the hydrofoil's most vociferous critics and the data obtained laid firm foundations for many of the second generation, high performance, seagoing vessels of today.

It was at about this time, in the mid-1950's, that the US Navy began to play what was to become a dominant role in hydrofoil development. Spasmodic interest had been displayed by the US Department of the Navy since the beginning of the century, but more recently it had been greatly stimulated by the success of von Schertel's developments and Hook's demonstrations. The chief reasons for the US Navy's renewed interest lay in its concern to improve the speed of its surface units in order to keep pace with the ever-increasing speed of other types of weaponry. In particular, it was hoped that hydrofoils would provide a more effective platform for coping with the high-speed, continuously submerged, nuclear submarine.

Vessels with fully submerged foils are the only craft capable of sustaining water speeds higher than those of fast submarines in heavy seas. Until the introduction of such vessels, a submarine operating under the cover of moderate-to-heavy seas had far greater tactical flexibility than either conventional surface craft or ASW aircraft operating from carriers. Operating at a constant power level and weight, a hydrofoil of the size of NATO's 230-ton PHM loses relatively little speed with sea-state. In sea-state 6, its speed would only be reduced from about 50 to 44 knots. However in the same conditions, the speed of a conventional destroyer would drop from 37 knots to less than 10 knots. Another point in the hydrofoil's favour is that it presents a smaller and faster target in the event of torpedo attacks. Later, the US Navy, together with the navies of several other NATO countries, also came to regard the hydrofoil as an effective defence against the fast missile-craft and destroyers, which shadow the aircraft carriers and other major combat ships of the US 6th Fleet in the Mediterranean.

From 1947–60, the US Office of Naval Research, supported by the Bureau of Ships, sponsored many research and development projects, all directed towards the establishment of feasibility and basic design criteria. Theoretical analyses and model experiments were made and tests were conducted on a number of small craft.

One of the first vessels to employ an electronic autopilot was the Lantern, designed by Dr Vannevar Bush, who during World War II had played a major role in the development of the atomic bomb. It used a converted Sperry A-12 Gyropilot which controlled the craft in roll, pitch and yaw. Instead of the sonic height or sonic/radar sensor, which is employed almost exclusively in current craft, the Lantern employed a static pressure-sensing probe to maintain constant foil depth. While not a great success —its speed was less than 20 knots—it demonstrated the feasibility of employing a gyroscope-based control system for stabilisation.

There followed a number of other research craft, among them

a revised version of the Hook Halobates, and the Flying DUKW for the US Army, both built by Miami Shipbuilding Corporation, and Sealegs, basically a Chris-Craft boat with an automatic control system, designed jointly by Gibbs and Cox and the Flight Control Laboratory of the Massachusetts Institute of Technology.

Sealegs proved an outstanding success. A 5-ton craft with a fully-submerged canard foil system, it had a seagoing performance well in advance of that of any other craft of its size, and before long had provided sufficient data to convince the Office of Naval Research of the feasibility of the large submerged foil craft, which would greatly enhance the effectiveness of naval units. As a result, in 1960 emergency funds were made available to support an expanded research and development programme. Funds were allocated for the design and construction of the Boeing PCH-1 High Point, a 110-ton patrol boat intended primarily as an offshore ASW craft, and employing a scaled-up version of the foils employed on Sealegs.

At about the same time as the introduction of the Navy's accelerated programme, the US Maritime Administration, encouraged by the results of the Navy's research, decided that they, too, would explore the possibility of increasing the speed of sea transport through the use of hydrofoil ships.

The result was the gas-turbine powered HS Denison, named after the late Colonel Charles R. Denison, who initiated the commercial hydrofoil studies for the Administration. The vessel, built by Grumman Aircraft Engineering Corporation, was an 80-ton, 60-knot craft with surface-piercing main foils and a submerged aft foil. The Denison, which first became foilborne in 1962, was the first hydrofoil intended for operational use to be equipped with autopilot-controlled foils. It had a stability augmentation system, developed by Hamilton Standard, which actuated flaps on the main foil and varied the incidence of the stern foil. Hamilton Standard also supplied the autostabilisation system for the Boeing PCH-1 which was launched the following year.

In 1962, funds were made available for the design and construction of the Grumman AGEH-1 Plainview, a 320-ton experimental ASW hydrofoil and at the time of writing, the world's largest. This vessel was built to operate at subcavitating speeds of less than 60 knots, but the design provided for a subsequent doubling of power and the replacement of the foils by those of high-speed type. The hull was therefore designed to withstand wave impact at 90 knots!

In early 1966, contracts were placed with Grumman and Boeing for two 60-ton patrol gunboat hydrofoils, the PGH-1 Flagstaff with a controllable-pitch, super-cavitating propeller employing a Z-drive, and PGH-2 Tucumcari propelled by water-jets. The craft were built to an operational requirement which grew out of the need for high performance gunboats at the time of the Cuban missile crisis. They underwent combat evaluation as part of the Vietnam coastal surveillance force between September 1969 and February 1970. This exercise showed that both craft could operate in sea-states twice that required in their design specifications and that because of their smoother ride, mainten-ance was lower than that of comparable conventional vessels.

Of the two vessels, the Tucumcari, helped by the novelty and relative simplicity of its waterjet propulsion system, plus its trouble-free operation off Vietnam, attracted the most attention. In 1971 its capabilities were demonstrated once again, this time to NATO, in Europe. The result was that the Italian navy decided to order a derivative—the Swordfish—which is about to go into production.

While most NATO navies contended that the Tucumcari was far too small for their particular needs, many displayed a strong interest in very much larger craft employing the same formula. When in 1971 the US Navy proposed building a 230-ton fast patrol boat to combat the threat posed in the Mediterranean by missile-armed craft of the Osa and Komar types, Italy and the Federal Republic of Germany decided to become partners with the US Navy in a project to develop the craft, now known as the NATO PHM (Patrol Hydrofoil Missile) Programme. The US Navy has indicated that it will order twenty-five PHMs, the German Federal Republic is to buy ten, and the Italians one US-built craft, with others to be built in Italy. Interested observers in the PHM project include the navies of Canada, Australia, Denmark, the Netherlands, France and the United Kingdom.

According to senior officials of the US Naval Sea Systems Command, the next step is the development of a 1,100–1,300-ton destroyer escort hydrofoil with the ability to cross oceans without refuelling. Boeing's design team, which has already prepared preliminary designs for such a craft, feel that the technology associated with a 50-knot hydrofoil is now complete, and without any significant new research such a craft could be developed without difficulty.

Sealegs, then, had marked a turning point in the history of fully-submerged foil craft. The concept of the fully-submerged, autostabilised canard hydrofoil has since developed, step-by-step from the little Chris-Craft 5-tonner, via High Point, Tucumcari and the 230-ton PHM to the 1,300-ton destroyer-size vessel of the 1980's. In fact studies have been made employing exactly the same formula for craft of up to 4,400 tons. Two commercial craft have also employed this same approach, the Victoria, a 75-seater designed by Gibbs & Cox Inc., and the more recent 250-passenger Boeing Jetfoil. The Victoria, which cruises at 37–40 knots, was one of the first commercial hydrofoils to be certified by the US Coast Guard to carry passengers on Puget Sound.

If the inauguration of the world's first scheduled passenger service on Lake Maggiore in May 1953 marked the birth of the commercial hydrofoil, then May 1974 marked its 'coming of age'. In the ensuing twenty-one years, it had graduated from a minor tourist attraction to a mode of transport used annually by well over 25 million commuters and tourists in almost forty countries. Today there are just over 1,000 hydrofoils operating throughout the world, some 80 per cent. of which are employed in the Soviet Union. Most of those operating outside Russia employ foils of Supramar design, and these have now logged more than three billion passenger miles without a single fatal accident being recorded.

By 1975, orders for commercial craft were growing at a rate which manufacturers described as 'unprecedented'. In the Western World more new craft—from small runabouts to 500-seaters—were being designed, built or tested than ever before, and in the Soviet Union, consideration was being given to the setting up of a yard on the Black Sea to handle exclusively the building of hydrofoils for export. The industry is now rated as being both viable and successful and is expected to emerge as one of the most profitable sections of the shipbuilding industry within a decade.

# CHAPTER TWO

# DEFEATING THE WATER BARRIER

By the end of the nineteenth century, a number of engineers and inventors had set their minds to the task of introducing long overdue improvements in basic ship design. Before long it had become clear that the most practical way of beating the natural water speed barrier lay in circumventing the drag caused by a ships's hull by lifting it bodily out of the water while under way. Also, in the interest of comfort, there had to be a means of uncoupling the hull from the continual motion of the waves.

The early experiments undertaken by Porter, Hans Dineson, Thomamhul, Forlanini, Crocco and others, marked the beginnings of two totally new and different ship concepts—air-cushion vehicles and hydrofoils. The air-cushion vehicle raises itself clear of the water on either a static or dynamic cushion of air, and the hydrofoil rides on the hydrodynamic pressure differences created between the upper and lower sides of a foil as it moves through the water. Both concepts can take on a number of different shapes and, not suprisingly, confusion in identifying the various ACV and hydrofoil types occurs frequently. However, study will show that each individual design has its own distinctive features.

## Air-cushion vehicles

There are two main types of air-cushion vehicles, those raised above their supporting surface by a self-generated cushion of air and those that depend on forward speed to develop lift in much the same way as aircraft. The former are known as aerostatic and the latter as aerodynamic.

Aerostatic-type air-cushion vehicles are divided into two categories—plenum chamber craft and peripheral or annular jet craft. Plenum chamber craft employ the simplest of all surface effect concepts. Air is forced from the lift fan or fans directly into a recessed base—shaped like a bell or an inverted pudding basin—where it forms a cushion of pressurised air which causes the craft to rise to its designed hoverheight. Air is pumped into the chamber in sufficient volume to replace that leaking out beneath the base.

Today's plenum craft have a flexible fabric extension hung between the hardstructure and the surface to give increased obstacle and overwave clearance capability. Variants include the sidewall ACV, in which the air cushion is contained between solid sidewalls, or skegs, and transverse skirts fore and aft, and the Bertin-designed Naviplanes and Terraplanes, which employ separately-fed multiple plenum chambers, each surrounded by lightweight flexible skirts or jupes (petticoats). Because of their relatively simple design and construction, skirted plenum chamber craft are greatly favoured by light ACV enthusiasts, especially those who specialise in home design and construction.

Finally, there is the peripheral or annular jet type which is based on Sir Christopher Cockerell's original hovercraft principle. In this, the cushion is generated and sustained by a continuous jet of air expelled through ducts around the outer periphery of the base of the craft hardstructure. The flexible skirts fitted to this type can take the form either of an extension fitted to the outer wall of the air duct only, or an extension to both inner and outer walls.

## Aerodynamic craft

Aerodynamic craft include the ram-wing and the wing-in-ground-effect machine. The ram-wing is, in effect, a craft with a short-span wing with sidewalls at its tips. Its trailing edge and sidewalls remain either in contact with, or almost touching the water surface. At speed, lifting forces are generated both by the wing and the ram-air pressure built up beneath. The wing-in-ground-effect machine—known in the Soviet Union as the Ekranoplan—generally has the appearance of a flying-boat with short-span wings. It is designed to operate low down, at a height equal to half its wing span or less, where it rides on a dynamic air cushion set up between the machine and the surface below.

Flying within surface-effect, there is a remarkable drop in induced drag, which lowers fuel consumption, and increases the payload, or the range, by at least half as much again. The advantages of using the ground effect cushion were discovered as far back as fifty years ago when it helped the pilots of early commercial planes to extend their range when crossing the South Atlantic. RAF and Fleet Air Arm pilots in World War II frequently depended on the phenomenon to make their way to a friendly coastline when their craft were damaged or fuel was running low.

One of the world's leading designers of this class of air-cushion vehicle is Dr Alexander Lippisch, 'father' of the delta wing, and designer of the fastest fighter of World War II, the rocket-powered Me 163. One important characteristic of his Aerofoil boat, or 'winged hull' concept, is that by employing an inverted delta wing of low aspect-ratio, he has overcome pitch instability, one of the major problems encountered when flying close to the surface in a craft equipped with conventional wings. The normal behaviour is for the centre of pressure to travel rearwards as the surface is approached, causing the nose of the craft to pitch downwards. Dr Lippisch's inverted delta-wing configuration overcomes this tendency and is inherently stable in ground effect automatically maintaining a fixed height above the surface. Its degree of stability is such that both light and medium-size craft employing this concept can fly in and out of ground effect whenever necessary in order to clear shipping, shorelines and port installations, bends in rivers, bridges and fogbanks. In full flight these craft manoeuvre in exactly the same way as slow-flying aircraft, but once out of ground effect their economic advantages are lost, since in order to gain and maintain height, they have to operate at increased power.

## Flexible skirts

The hovercraft, without the invention of the skirt, could not have advanced far beyond the stage of an interesting idea. In general, skirts have deepened the air cushion for a given lift power by a factor of ten and reduced the size of a craft required to operate in a particular sea-state by 75 per cent. The considerable savings realised are perhaps best illustrated by comparing the sizes of craft, both skirted and unskirted, that would be required to operate across the English Channel, where the significant wave height is 8ft. The all-up weight of a vessel large enough and powerful enough to attain an 8-ft clearance height without a skirt would be in the region of 700–800 tons. The use of skirts on today's SR.N4 means that the all-up weight has only to be 200 tons. In addition the power required for the larger, skirtless craft would be in the region of 54,400 shp—four times the total output of the four Proteus gas-turbines on the SR.N4.

The leading names in skirt design and fabrication are FPT Products Ltd, a subsidiary of British Hovercraft Corporation,

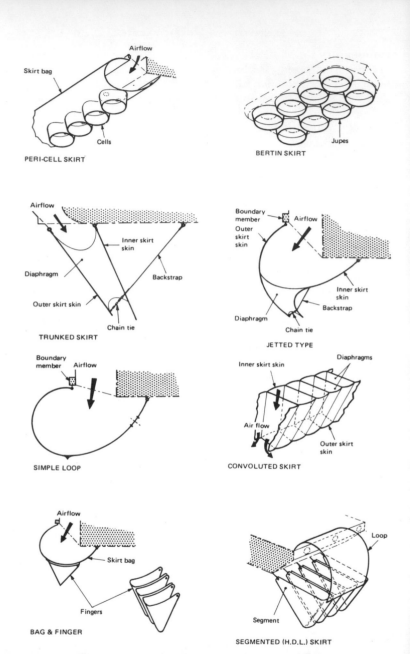

*Skirts in current use* (with acknowledgements to BHC).

Hovercraft Development Ltd, Avon Rubber Co, Air Cushion Equipment Ltd and the Northern Rubber Company. After earlier experiments with simple bag and trunked skirts, BHC in 1965 decided to concentrate on those of the 'fingered-bag' type. Pressurised air from the lift fan is fed firstly into the bag and then bled via air exit holes to the underside of the craft to form the cushion. At the bottom of the bag, beneath each exit hole, is an open-faced finger or segment which channels air inwards towards the centre of the craft base. Fingers were first introduced in order to reduce wave drag and spray. But they also take most of the skirt wear and tear, thus helping to reduce maintenance costs. Initially, the depth of the fingers in relation to the total skirt depth was about 30 per cent. but this has been increased to as much as 50 per cent.

Originally, craft like the SR.N4 and SR.N6 were operated with a 1.5 degree bow-up trim to avert the possibility of severe decelerations should the front skirts 'pick up'. As a result the stern fingers experienced considerably more wear than those at the bow. Those fitted aft had a life span of about 100 hours compared with about 500 hours for the bow fingers. In 1972, largely as a result of studies conducted by BHC and British Rail on the SR.N4s and SR.N6s, a new tapered skirt was introduced. The skirt at the bow was deepened by about 2 ft 6 in. to maintain the necessary one degree bow-up trim, then tapered all the way back to the original skirt depth at the rear. This means that the craft now sits within a skirt designed to have a $1\frac{1}{2}$ degree bow-up attitude. As a result there has been a marked decrease in finger wear at the stern on both designs.

A notable feature of the BHC fingered-bag skirts is the use of cushion compartmentation for additional stability. On the SR.N6 this takes the form of a longitudinal keel and twin athwartship stability bags, while on the much larger SR.N4, the cushion has only three compartments, the longitudinal keel extending only from the stern up to the athwartship dividers. By employing compartmentation, a relatively high degree of pitch and roll stiffness can be achieved which prevents excessive water contact.

Under certain adverse conditions, it is possible for the bow skirt to contact the surface, progressively build-up drag, and then produce a nose-down pitching moment. Unless controlled, severe decelerations of the craft, known as 'plough-in', follows, and this can lead to a serious loss of stability and possibly an overturning moment. As the outer edge of the bow skirt drags towards the centre of the craft (termed 'tuck-under') there is a sharp reduction in the righting moment of the cushion pressure. As the downward pitch angle increases, the stern tends to rise from the surface and excessive yawing develops. Considerable deceleration takes place down to hump speed and the danger of a roll over in a small craft is accentuated by following waves with further increase of the pitch angle.

To help overcome the problems of 'tuck-under' and 'plough-in', BHC has raised the skirt hinge lines on both the SR.N4 Mk 2 and the BH.7. On the former, an 'anti-plough' bag is incorporated in the bow skirt. This is sealed since it gives the required resistance to water impact and prevents 'tuck-under' and 'plough-in'. The bow skirt on the BH.7 bulges outwards on contact with the water, thereby delaying 'tuck-under' and providing a righting moment.

SR.N4s operate in 3–4-ft seas at 50 knots and more, and the frequency of skirt impact under these conditions is far worse than that experienced by motor vehicle tyres under cross-country conditions. The degree of finger wear is illustrated by the experience of Hoverlloyd Ltd which operates three SR.N4s between Ramsgate (Pegwell Bay) and Calais. Each year the company's craft operate a total of 4,000 hours and consume some 1,500 fingers. Skirt fingers are therefore a major cost item in ACV operation, to which of course has to be added the cost of man hours to make the necessary repairs and finger changes.

Research is being undertaken into materials and processes that will increase the wear resistance of fingers. Finger wear is generally felt to be a function of speed. Finger wear rate is highest in medium sea conditions at 50 knots. In smoother conditions there are fewer impacts, so the wear rate reduces, and in rougher conditions, when the operating speed is reduced to 30–40 knots, wear rate is reduced once again.

One current approach towards the development of better materials is aimed at the use of lighter and more flexible fabrics. There is evidence to support the theory that, due to their flexibility, they offer the least resistance to water drag.

A major skirt design based on this theory is Hovercraft Development Ltd's segmented type. This is employed on the HD.2, the Vosper Thornycroft VT 1 and VT 2, the EM 2 and many new craft either under design or construction. It is also being employed for industrial applications, including heavy lift platforms of up to 750 tons gross weight, hoverpallets and hovertrailers. The skirt comprises an open loop with segments attached to the outer

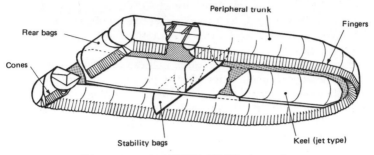

*Skirt system on the BHC SR.N6 Winchester class.*

edge and linked to the underside of the structure. There is no compartmentation within the cushion and since there is no restriction of the airflow between the loop of the skirt and the cushion, the pressure ratio between the two is much the same and therefore the internal power losses are small. Thin material is employed for fabricating the skirts and the resulting low inertia ensures a smooth ride. As the skirt segments occupy a substantial part of the full cushion depth, the system enables craft to clear high waves and obstacles. Another advantage offered by this skirt system is that the hardstructure of the craft employing this approach is chamfered all round so that the inner attachment points of the segments can be reached without jacking the craft up from its off-cushion position, thus simplifying maintenance.

BHC has found that the most successful skirt materials have been based on nylon or terylene core fabrics with coatings of either natural rubber or neoprene. Glass, cotton, rayon and even steel fabrics have been tried but were found unsatisfactory. Steel and glass were unable to stand up to the continual flagellation from the waves, while cotton and rayon had insufficient tear strength and durability. Amongst the coating compounds tried in the early days of skirt development were nitrile/PVC and polyurethane.

Skirts account for nearly 15 per cent. of the all-up weight of the 10-ton SR.N6 and 10 per cent. of that of the 200-ton SR.N4. Because of this, and in the interests of craft performance and payload, skirts are normally kept to the minimum size necessary for satisfactory operation. Skirt depth is generally the same as that of the significant wave height in the area in which the craft is to be operated. Tests have indicated that in the interests of craft stability, the skirt depth should not exceed 15–20 per cent. of the

cushion beam. The great majority of ACVs are capable of operating in waves of at least twice their skirt depth, particularly if
the waves are long and can be contoured without bow hardstructure impact.

The largest ACV manufacturer in France is SEDAM, which
holds the world licence for Bertin patents covering both the
Naviplane and Terraplane series. A feature of these designs is the
employment of the Bertin multiple plenum system, with air from
the lift fans being supplied to these either individually or in
groups. Each plenum has its own skirt or jupe and in turn these
are surrounded by a single 'labyrinth' skirt located around the
base of the hardstructure periphery.

The Pericell skirt, one of the latest of the skirt configurations,
combines features of the fingered bag skirt and the Bertin
arrangement of jupes, with large individual cells taking the place
of the fringe of fingers at the base of the skirt bag. The arrangement shows some improvement in static stability over the
fingered bag configuration. One of the first applications of this
type of skirt is on the SES-100A.

## *Motive power*

Power for an ACV's lift and propulsion system depends upon
the type of application envisaged for the particular design, its
size, the environment in which it will operate and the performance required. Other factors that have to be considered by both
the manufacturer and the operator are the engine's output,
weight, fuel consumption, overhaul life, likely maintenance
costs, availability of spares and the extent of the engine manufacturer's back-up facilities.

Air-cushion vehicle powerplants in use today range from the
converted drone, go-cart, outboard and motor-cycle petrol
engines employed in small runabouts and rally craft, to the four
3,400 shp Rolls-Royce Marine Proteus free-turbines employed
on the SR.N4. Between these extremes are the single 200 hp
Chrysler V8 car engine of the Sealand SH-2 six-seater, the three
Cummins water-cooled diesels of the Hovermarine HM.2 series,
and the single 1,000 shp Marine Gnome of the SR.N6 Mk 1s
58-seat passenger ferry.

At present, no engine manufacturer has found the demand for
ACV engines sufficient to justify the development of specific
designs for this purpose. Consequently, all ACV prime movers

in use at present are adapted from standard designs, using marinised versions wherever these exist, since these will have had many components treated to withstand the corrosive effects of salt-laden air.

Gas-turbine powered craft designed to operate in a marine environment have thick, loosely woven pads of either metal or plastic wire fitted in the engine air intakes to filter out water and solid particles from the engine air. As a further precaution against the ingestion of salt and sand particles into the engine, it is also common practice to take engine air from the lift-fan plenum chamber.

Because of its very low weight per unit of power (lb/hp) and favourable power/speed performance, the gas-turbine engine is the first choice of the manufacturer for most craft of 8–10 tons and upwards. However, many water transport operators in under-developed countries would select a diesel-powered craft in preference to one with gas-turbines because of its lower fuel requirements, operating and maintenance costs. Another consideration is that since skilled diesel engineers are more readily available than trained gas-turbine engineers, they are easier to recruit.

Although certain of today's high-speed, lightweight diesels are suitable for smaller commercial and military ACVs of up to about 25 tons gross weight, the free-turbine versions of aircraft gas-turbines are the only prime movers which will meet the power and weight requirements of larger craft. The projected 2,000-ton SES for the US Navy will be powered by six 20,000 shp GE LM-2,500 gas-turbines; two driving the lift fans and four for the waterjet propulsion systems. These are amongst the most powerful gas-turbines in the world, but in order to drive the follow-on generation of US Navy SESs, the all-up weight of which could be around 12,500 tons, at least four times as much power will be required for propulsion alone.

It is estimated that these vessels will each require about 315,000 hp to propel them over the peaks of hump drag which would occur at about 42 knots. High-speed and long-range require large amounts of energy. The substantial fuel requirements and costs are factors which led the United States Government to conduct studies into the feasibility of nuclear powerplants in large surface-effect ships. Much of the research to date has been conducted under the direction of Mr Frank E. Rom at the National Aeronautics and Space Administration's Lewis Research Center, Cleveland, Ohio.

The nuclear powerplant studies by NASA for SES application would be similar in design to that proposed for aircraft propulsion. The reactor, which is surrounded by a containment vessel and shielding, heats a fluid, such as high pressure helium, which is ducted to a heat exchanger located between the combustors and compressor of a typical ducted fan engine. The engine can then operate on the heat transferred by the heat exchanger or by the combustion of fuel in the conventional chambers.

Measures to ensure the complete safety of the reactor have been examined in depth. The containment vessel surrounding the reactor is designed to prevent entirely the release of fissionable products following the worst conceivable accident or a reactor meltdown. The materials employed in the shield are designed not only to withstand the shock of an impact but also to distribute uniformly the heat generated during a meltdown.

The savings in terms of fuel costs are considerable since the price of nuclear fuel is only about one-third or one-sixth of chemical fuel, and reliable reactors could be built that will operate for 10,000 hours without refuelling. Another attractive feature is that for large SESs of between 5–10,000 tons, the weight of the nuclear powerplant would be less than 10 per cent. of the gross weight. NASA believe that it would be possible to attain an operating cost of about 2 cents per ton-mile through the use of nuclear power. They say that, theoretically, it would take a 1,500 strong fleet of 10,000-ton SESs to handle 10 per cent. of the world trade which they estimate is the volume that could be 'captured' as a result of being able to reduce freight costs to 2 cents per ton-mile. The use of such craft could be even more attractive than the figures given, for they do not reflect the additional cargo traffic that would undoubtedly be attracted by the promise of low rates plus very much higher speeds.

## Lift systems

Lift fans are responsible for providing an ACV with adequate cushion air. Often they are considered the heart and lungs of this type of vehicle, since the ACV is essentially an air-blowing system which has been designed to lift and move a given payload. The fan pumps a large and continuous volume of pressurised air into the cavity beneath the vehicle where it diffuses to form the cushion which then lifts the craft to the steady-state condition. At this point the air being discharged into the cushion is just

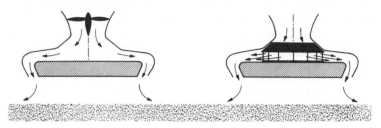

Left: *An axial-flow lift fan generates an airflow that is* parallel *to the axis of rotation.* Right: *The centrifugal-flow cushion lift fan generates an airflow at* right angles *to the axis of rotation.*

sufficient to replace that escaping from around the periphery.

Generally speaking, the larger the craft, the greater its cushion flow and cushion pressure, although much depends on the configuration, weights and duties of the individual designs. Today's smallest fully-amphibious commercial craft require about 10–15 psf cushion pressure and 100–200 cfs cushion flow, and the largest need 60–70 psf cushion pressure and 27,000 cfs cushion flow.

Most of the fans in current use are either of axial-flow or centrifugal flow type, although mixed-flow systems, employing features of both, have been successful in several instances. The axial fan, like a conventional aircraft propeller, moves air in a direction parallel to the axis of rotation, while the centrifugal fan traps air between its blades then throws it outwards radially through centrifugal acceleration.

Axial fans are mainly employed in vertical ducts, and impel air downwards directly into the cushion. Their relative simplicity and availability has led to them being used extensively by the makers of small plenum craft, particularly of the homebuilt variety, but due to their relatively low airflow capacity, they have to be operated at high-speed, resulting in a high tip speed which means they are inclined to be noisy.

For bigger craft, in which air has to be distributed throughout the length and breadth of a large plenum chamber before discharging into the cushion, the centrifugal fan displays significant advantages. It develops greater static pressure at lower tip speeds, handles a higher volume of airflow, is simple to build, easier to install and is more robust in service. Nevertheless, in the ceaseless quest for greater comfort and efficiency, designers have not lost sight of the possibility of using multiple variable-pitch axial fans on ocean-going ACVs, not only for providing lift air, but also as a means of controlling craft heave. An analysis of the full spectrum of wave forces has been undertaken, and in the low frequency areas, where most of the wave energy is found, it is theoretically possible to counter heave by fan-pitch change rates comparable to those of the variable-pitch airscrews employed on aircraft. Studies suggest that heave accelerations could be reduced by more than four-fold and the craft motion brought well within established comfort levels.

## Propulsion

Few forms of propulsion for ACVs have been left untried. Those employed so far have ranged from sails to air propellers and from waterscrews to waterjets. As may be expected, the type of propulsion employed on any vehicle is governed by the vehicle's application and the overall performance which has to be achieved. Air propulsion of one type or another is a more logical choice for an amphibious vehicle, while waterjets or waterscrews are more likely to be specified for vessels designed to operate entirely over water.

The forms in current use or proposed for the future include:

| *Air Propulsion* | *Water Propulsion* |
|---|---|
| Air propellers | Water propeller |
| Shrouded air propeller | Waterjet |
| Airjet | Paddlewheel |
| Turbofan | Towed by helicopter |
| Gas-turbine jet | |
| Sails | |
| Towed by helicopter | |
| *Ground Contact Propulsion* | *Tracked Skimmers* |
| Wheels | Air propeller |
| Caterpillar drive | Gas-turbine jet |
| Pushed by hand | Turbofan |
| Towed by tractor | Linear induction motor |
| Towed by horse | |

In spite of the many alternatives given, more than 90 per cent. of today's ACVs are propelled by propellers, and most of the remaining craft derive their thrust from waterscrews or waterjets. However, the trend towards hydrodynamic propulsion or hybrid systems is likely to grow, since if one examines the propulsion needs of a 10,000 ton SEV required to operate at 100 knots, it would have to be fitted with either ten air propellers, each of 60 ft diameter, or ten high bypass fans of 35 ft diameter.

To obtain a corresponding amount of thrust by hydrodynamic means alone, would require only two 30-ft diameter super-cavitating propellers or four 12-ft diameter waterjets. In other words, extremely large and sometimes impractical air-propeller areas are required as vessels become larger, while generally speaking, hydrodynamic systems for the same shaft horsepower remain a practical proposition in terms of actual size. A reduction in air propeller diameters results in a drop in efficiency due to the reduction in mass airflow rates, which means a corresponding increase in shaft horsepower requirements. Although inconvenient as a source of thrust for ship-size craft because of the large numbers required, air-propellers are, nevertheless, the most efficient form of propulsion for ACVs at speeds of 150 mph and above. However, in terms of performance, they cannot compare with the water use of propellers or waterjets at low speeds. Tests made with another form of air propulsion—shrouded propellers —indicate that these offer a better low-speed performance, but the shrouds add substantially to unit weight and their drag means a marked reduction in efficiency at speeds over 100 knots.

The most promising solution so far for large, high-speed craft is an arrangement employing high bypass fans for high speeds in combination with semi-submerged supercavitating propellers to take it up through the hump speed to 70–80 knots. The chief advantage of the high bypass fan is that while its performance is comparable to that of an air-propeller, it is only half the diameter. Additional attractions are that it weighs substantially less, is quieter in operation and can be adapted to a variety of different kinds of installation. A wide range of high bypass fans of up to 40,000 hp output is expected to become available from the air-craft industry over the next few years as the wide-fuselage 'jumbo' concept develops.

The SES design projects revealed so far employ rigid sidewalls which are ideal for housing either waterjet pumps or waterscrews and their drives. Since the lower parts of the sidewalls are immersed in the water, either for stability or directional control, the propulsor is located at the extreme end of the sidewall. The US Navy's two 100-ton sidewalls test craft, the SES-100A and SES-100B were designed to operate at speeds of 70–80 knots. The SES-100A is the first air-cushion vehicle capable of such performance deriving its thrust from waterjet propulsion, while the SES-100B is the first 80-knot craft to be equipped with semi-submerged supercavitating propellers. Undoubtedly both systems have considerable development potential but it is unlikely that the top speeds currently attainable, by the use of either method, can be greatly increased. In the case of water propellers, the current short life of propellers due to cavitation erosion will almost certainly be extended by both the use of more highly resistant metals and improved designs, but efficiency losses will almost certainly remain.

The use of a partially submerged propeller driven through the sidewall transom on the SES-100B was an attractive approach, since it avoided the need for a propeller shaft, supports and bearings and also the significant drag they would have created. The efficiency of the propeller was found to be similar to that of a fully submerged propeller, the thrust and torque produced being proportional to the submerged propeller disc area.

There is general agreement among marine propulsion experts that supercavitating propellers can be developed that will enable speeds of 100 knots to be attained. Approaches include a wedge-shaped propeller employing a sharp leading edge and square trailing edge, causing an upper surface cavity which collapses well downstream of the blade section. Another idea is a variable-camber supercavitating marine propeller which promises to offer improvements similar to those demonstrated by variable-pitch aircraft propellers. By adjusting the camber, the helmsman would be able to provide optimum thrust for take-off, cruising and sprint performance. Hamilton Standard's variable camber propeller has blades which are segmented in the centre in such a way as to permit individual adjustment of the two sections.

When a vessel's speed exceeds 45 knots, the use of super-cavitating propellers becomes a necessity. Early on in the US Navy's hydrofoil experiments, it was found that at 45–50 knots, the bronze aft propellers on the PCH-1 were seriously eroded by cavitation on both faces and required replacement or repair after about 40 hours of operation. Cast alloys employing much harder metals have been used since then. Titanium and its alloys are in demand because of their high strength, high cavitation and corrosion resistance. The first vessels so equipped were the HS Denison and the 320-ton AGEH-1 Plainview which has two four-bladed titanium propellers, each of 5 ft diameter.

## Waterjets

The waterjet is one of the oldest known concepts for marine propulsion. The first patent was granted to two Englishmen, Toogood and Hayes in 1661. It was re-introduced by Benjamin Franklin in 1775 and first used in 1782, when James Ramsey employed them to propel a passenger ferry across the Potomac between Washington and Alexandria. In terms of propulsive efficiency, however, the waterjet is inferior to the marine propeller, and development has been spasmodic. Applications of waterjet propulsion over the years had been limited to relatively low-cost pleasure craft and amphibious military vehicles, until Boeing, in 1963, introduced its Little Squirt gas-turbine, waterjet powered testbed. Boeing's interest in this form of propulsion lay primarily in establishing an alternative to the supercavitating propeller and the extremely expensive Z-drive system previously considered necessary for hydrofoils designed to fly in high waves. Little Squirt, equipped with an off-the-shelf double-suction centrifugal pump, achieved the surprisingly high propulsive coefficient of 0.48 at a speed of 50 knots.

It was largely due to Boeing's confidence in waterjets, that the US Navy came to consider it as an alternative to supercavitating marine propellers for the SES-100A. Although the research and test programmes undertaken with waterjets have led to the construction of easily operated and reliable units, the hydrodynamic difficulties caused by cavitation in ducts and pumps, and the need to design variable area inlets, still present serious design problems. Broaching of the inlets, ship motion in heave and pitch, and the mechanical adjustment of the inlets to avoid cavitation at speeds up to 80 knots, are factors which are undergoing continuous research to make the 100-knot plus surface-effect ship a reality.

The latest form of ACV marine propulsion to undergo serious study is also the oldest—the paddlewheel. Chief protagonist of this type of propulsion is Sir Christopher Cockerell, who is currently working on a large area, wave-contouring, water-stroking propulsion system specifically devised for hovercraft. By the use of feathering, Sir Christopher's system is able to compress the 20-ft diameter, Mississippi-type wheel into a modern counterpart of only 5 ft diameter. To power a 2,000-tonner requires 150 sq. ft of immersed blade area. Sir Christopher states that his wheel can provide this with a blade immersion of only 2 ft, the total width of the units amounting to some 75 ft. The wheels would be mounted on a trailing arm enabling them to contour the waves. Height sensors, forward of the wheels, would provide a phase-lead for the control signals. Certainly the approach is ingenious and offers some unique advantages. Among its attractions are low noise, shallow immersion, ease of access for servicing, low thrustline and good headwind performance. Moreover, it would enable a 2–5,000 ton craft to operate in shallow water and propel itself up a beach for loading or servicing. However, it remains to be seen if this type of propulsion can meet the demand for 100 knots. At present, the only air-cushion craft with marine propellers to meet this requirement is the Lippisch Aero Skimmer —a derivative of his Aerofoil Boat—which has attained more than 150 knots during tests.

The subject of Tracked Skimmers and their propulsion systems is covered in Chapter Five. The most popular ACV ground-drive system is wheeled propulsion although, as the demand for these vehicles grows in northern and Arctic terrain, caterpillar tracks are coming into use more and more. Typical of the Bertin Terraplane wheeled-drive vehicle range is the T3S, which is being marketed in French-speaking Central Africa for use over unprepared land regardless of the season or the state of the soil. A combined ground-effect machine and four-wheeled vehicle, it is driven like a car or truck, but with the essential difference that it can be run at speeds up to 31 mph (50 km/h) over mud, uneven ground or water. A hydraulic system allows the transference from the air cushion to the road wheels from 20–50 per cent. of the gross weight, according to the nature of the ground surface and gradient. Both Bertin and the Ashley Institute, Belfast, are studying track-laying air-cushion vehicles (TLACVs) with tracks in the form of a broad belt that loops around the entire lower chassis including the air cushion, underneath the load platform.

The first air-cushion (crawler) tractor to be employed operationally was the MVP-3, designed and built by the Tyumen/ West Siberian branch of the All-Union Oil Machinery Research Institute. Cushion air is fed into a skirt hung between two crawler tracks which provide propulsion, steering and support on hard surfaces. As with the Bertin T3S, the cushion pressure is variable and the load is divided between the cushion and the tracks depending on the ground surface and the gradient. The vehicle, which is apparently a converted mobile battlefield rocket launcher, is capable of 50 mph over swamps and can cruise at 30 mph.

## Hydrofoils

After making her first crossing of the English Channel in an SR.N4, a well-known Frenchwoman—a journalist—found it almost impossible to believe that the giant hovercraft that had carried her all the way to Boulogne rode on a cushion of air. Her amazement, not to mention that of her editor, was reflected the next day in this classic headline: 'Captain Says Hovercraft Has Nothing Under Its Skirt'.

Unlike the ACV, with its invisible bubble of pressurised air, the hydrofoil's means of support is a very solid system of foils and struts fabricated in specially hardened alloys or corrosion resistant steel. Foils are small wings, almost identical to those of an aircraft, and designed in exactly the same way to generate lift. The foil systems in current use are basically either surface piercing, submerged or semi-submerged. There are a few craft with hybrid systems, the Supramar PT 150, for example, with a surface-piercing bow foil and an autostabilised, fully-submerged bow foil, and the de Havilland Canada FHE-400, which has a surface-piercing bow foil and a combined surface piercing and submerged foil aft.

### Surface-piercing

Surface-piercing foils are generally V-shaped although a few are trapeze or W-shaped, having either a horizontal or W configuration at the base instead of a classical V shape. The upper parts of the foils pierce the surface on either side. A feature of the V-foil, introduced by General Crocco and then developed over many years by Hanns von Schertel, is that it is area stabilised, and was the first type of foil to demonstrate inherent stability in any sea-state. The forces restoring normal trim are provided by the area of the foil that becomes submerged. When the craft rolls to one side, the immersion of increased foil area automatically causes additional lift to be generated which counters the roll and restores the craft back to an even keel again.

Pitching is countered in much the same way. A downward movement at the bow results in an increase in the submerged area of the forward foil. This generates additional lift which raises the bow to normal trim once more. As the craft speed increases, so increased lift is generated and the craft is raised further out of the water. In turn, this reduces the wetted area of the foil and thus the amount of hydrodynamic lift generated. Since the lift must be equal to the weight of the craft, and as the lift depends on the speed and the wetted foil area, the hull remains at a predetermined height above the water in a state of level flight.

Unquestionably, the surface-piercing foil has given excellent performance on inland waters, in coastal regions and within sheltered sea areas. It has natural stability, simplicity of construction, ease of handling and maintenance and considerable strength. However, for heavy sea conditions, a fully-submerged foil is superior because of its better performance in waves. One of the drawbacks of the conventional surface-piercing foil is that its natural stability tends to make it follow the up and down movement of waves, resulting in vertical, jolting acceleration which upsets both the passengers and crew. Ideally, instead of contouring over these waves, it should platform through them while maintaining a level flight path. But unfortunately, it has no method of distinguishing whether the bow is falling or a rising wave is being encountered, so additional lift is generated in both cases. In the second case, however, there is the risk that if the wave is not of the right length and shape, a major part of the foil will rise above the surface, resulting in a loss of lift and causing the craft to crash down on to its hull.

The main problem lies in its poor performance in a following sea. In these conditions, since it is travelling faster than the waves, it overtakes them from behind. When climbing up the back of these waves, the orbital, or circular motion, of the water particles within the waves will be falling downwards. This reduces the velocity of flow over the foil, which loses lift, causing the craft to drop on to its hull. When the craft encounters a head sea, the situation is, of course, reversed. The limiting wave height for most V-foiled craft in following seas is three-quarters that for head seas. It soon became clear that for heavy and following seas, the fully submerged foil would be superior. In addition to possessing automatic depth control, a stabilisation system could be built into it which meant that here was an opportunity to limit rolling and pitching moments and vertical accelerations for the very first time.

## Submerged foils

As their name suggests, submerged foils are located completely below the air/water interface, at depths where the orbital motion of the waves is considerably reduced. However, as they cannot tell which direction is up and which is down, they have to be instructed how to respond by motion sensing devices. Since the vessel sits on top of relatively small foils, it is top heavy. If its altitude and attitude were not checked continually and adjusted, it would crash down on its hull. To ensure that such a mishap is averted, a sonic, radar, mechanical or air stabilisation system has to be installed to maintain the foils at the correct depth and the craft at its proper attitude. It is also responsible for controlling the craft from the moment of take-off to touchdown, in heave, when the craft rises, vertically in response to wave motion, and about all three axes—pitch, roll and yaw. The system must also ensure that the craft makes co-ordinated, banked turns, in heavy seas to reduce the side-loads on the foil struts; ensure that vertical and lateral accelerations are kept within limits to prevent excessive loads on the structure and finally, ensure a smooth ride for the crew and passengers.

In sonic, radar and mechanical systems, the stabilising control forces are generated in a manner similar to that employed on aircraft, by the deflection of flaps or elevators at the trailing edges of the foils or by varying the incidence angle of the entire foil.

A typical automatic control system is that employed on the Boeing Jetfoil, a 45-knot waterjet-propelled commercial hydrofoil with an all-up weight of 106 long tons. The system senses the motion and position of the craft through the use of its gyros, accelerometers and two sonic height sensors at the bow. Signals from all of these are combined in a control computer with manual commands from the helm of the craft. The resulting computer outputs provide control surface deflections through electro-hydraulic servo actuators. Lift control is provided by full span trailing edge flaps on each foil. Forward and aft flaps operate differentially to provide pitch variation and height control, and the aft flaps operate differentially to provide roll control for changes of direction.

The system introduces the correct degree of bank and steering to co-ordinate the turn in full and ensure that the foil tips do not broach the surface and introduce ventilation. Turn rates of 6 degrees a second are attained within 5 seconds of providing a basic change command at the helm. Only three basic controls are employed for foilborne operation. The throttle is used to set the speed, the height command lever to set the required foil depth and the helm to set the required heading. If a constant course is required, a 'heading hold' circuit accomplishes this automatically.

For take-off, the foil depth is set, the throttles for the two 3,300 shp Allison free-powered gas-turbines advanced, and the hull clears the water in about 60 seconds. Acceleration continues until the craft automatically stabilises at the required depth and the speed dictated by the particular throttle setting. The throttle setting is reduced for landing, the craft settling as the speed drops. The speed normally diminishes from 45 knots (cruising speed) to 15 knots in about 30 seconds. In emergencies, more rapid landings can be made by the use of the height command lever to make water contact within 2 seconds.

The control system is very similar to that employed on the US Navy's PCH Mod 1, PGH-2, Tucumcari, AGEH and PHM and employs the same modular construction techniques. Components utilised are all well-proven items of aerospace hardware, selected for their success in aircraft autopilots. The controller on the PHM is based almost exclusively on aircraft-type fittings, including solid-state computers, tubing and valves, power to operate the flaps and forward strut/rudder being supplied by hydraulic components identical or similar to those used on the Boeing 747 'Jumbo' jet airliner.

The Jetfoil's designers were obviously able to benefit a great deal from the US Navy's PCH-1, PCH-Mod-1 and Tucumcari programmes, resulting in a commercial vessel that is almost certainly second to none in comfort and performance. One of the lessons learned from Tucumcari, for example, was the necessity to replace the single central heave accelerometer with twin units, one immediately above each main foil, so that flaps on each could be controlled individually, thus preventing the discomforting phenomenon known as 'roll jiggle', which was encountered in steep oblique seas when each aft foil was in a different part of a wave experiencing differing orbital forces.

One of the latest goals of the US Navy is to standardise hydrofoil autopilots, and to this end it instituted in 1972, the

Hydrofoil Universal Digital Autopilot Programme (HUDAP). The aim is to develop a highly reliable system which would have sufficient flexibility to be used on all present and future hydrofoils and the capacity to integrate the automatic control with other ship functions. The system, based on digital computers, will incorporate circuitry over and above that required for normal control tasks in order to take on additional responsibilities including the following:

navigation during automatic course or track keeping, or for automated and pre-programmed evasive manoeuvres;

obstacle avoidance;

fuel management, weight and balance control.

The most original approach to the problem of lift control is one devised by Supramar. It is a system based on the physical phenomenon that lift can be influenced by the admission of air to the foil upper surface—the low-pressure region— without resorting to moving foil parts. Lift is varied according to the quantity of air admitted through air exits along the upper surface, ducting the flow away from the foil section with an effect similar to that of a deflected flap. The air cavities extend behind the trailing edge, producing a virtual lengthening of the foil profile.

The quantity of air admitted is controlled by valves actuated by signals from a damped pendulum and a rate gyro. The pendulum causes the craft to right itself after heeling and ensures that it turns with co-ordinated banking. The gyroscope is mounted in such a way (Page 73) that it senses both pitch and roll and then restores normal trim through pneumatically amplified signals which operate simple push-pull rods to open and shut the air valves.

The system was first introduced on the Flipper, a Supramar PT 50 on which the normal surface-piercing aft foils were replaced by a fully submerged rear foil with air stabilisation vents. Flipper, in 3-ft waves, was found to be considerably more comfortable than similar vessels in 1-ft waves. It was then successfully employed on the PT 150 and PTS 75 Mk III.

In 1965, the US Navy awarded Supramar a contract for the construction of a 5-ton research craft, based on a PT 3 hull and redesigned ST 3A. The ST 3A was the first craft with fully submerged foils to be fitted with air stabilisation. During sea trials in the Mediterranean, it was tested at 54 knots and demonstrated that a fully-submerged craft can be stabilised and controlled by an air-feed system in both calm and rough water.

At a wave height of 3 ft (0.91 m.) or one-tenth of the boat length, vertical accelerations of only 0.08 g. were measured, which compares favourably with the sea test results for other craft with fully submerged foils. Supramar has incorporated the system in a design concept for a 250-ton patrol boat hydrofoil, which meets the tactical requirements established by the West German and other NATO navies.

Supramar is still developing air feed, both as a stabilisation system and as an aid to transiting from the subcavitating to the supercavitating mode without the sudden loss of lift experienced on a flapped foil with the onset of cavitation. Tests have shown that, with the influx of air, cavitation disappears entirely, or almost entirely, so that constant lift is available during the critical period of transition from steady, non-cavitating flow to super cavitation. Tank tests, under a contract from the US Navy, are being undertaken at the Netherlands Ship Model Basin, where sea-state conditions can be simulated and the test carriage speed is 60 knots.

As seagoing craft increase in size, so do their foils and control flaps. Under examination is the possibility of reducing the overall foil size by employing air feed lift control in conjunction with variable incidence foils, instead of trailing edge flaps.

## *Mechanical incidence control*

The first and most successful mechanically-operated incidence control system is the Hydrofin principle, designed by Christopher Hook, who pioneered this development of the fully-submerged foil. Reference was made to the major role he played in building the first successful fully-submerged foil craft in Chapter One.

On the Hydrofin, a fixed, high-riding crash-preventer subfoil is mounted ahead of and beneath the bow. This is only immersed when the craft is sitting on the water in displacement mode, and it also serves as a platform for mounting a lightweight pitch control sensor which is hinged to the rear. The sensor rides on the waves and continuously transmits wave height information through a connecting linkage to vary the angle of incidence of the main foils as necessary to maintain them at the required depth. A filter system is fitted to ensure that the hull is lifted over waves exceeding the height of the keel above water.

Roll control is provided by two additional sensors trailing aft of the main foil struts, port and starboard. The pilot has overriding control through a control column operated in the same way as that on an aircraft.

Another purely mechanical system is the Savitsky Flap, invented by Dr Daniel Savitsky of the Davidson Laboratory, Stevens Institute of Technology, New Jersey. Dr Savitsky's system is employed on Atlantic Hydrofoils' Sea World and Flying Cloud designs. Hinged vertical control flaps are used for foil lift variation. These are canted outwards and attached mechanically to the trailing edge of the foil struts. At the normal flying height only the lower part of the Savitsky flap is submerged. As a greater portion is submerged due to increased wave height, the pressure on the depth-sensing flap increases, causing it to turn and raise the foil flap, thus increasing lift and restoring normal in-flight attitude and flying height.

One of the most recent approaches to foil stabilisation is that employed by Dynafoil Inc., of Newport Beach, California, on their little Dynafoil Mark I two-seat runabout. The craft, a fibre-glass-hulled sports hydrofoil, is intended as a marine counterpart to the motorcycle and snowmobile, and has a fully submerged main foil aft and a small incidence-controlled twin-delta (biplane configuration) foil forward. The angle of incidence is controlled mechanically by a curved delta-shaped planing control foil, set at an inclined angle in such a way as to deflect upwards as the water pressure increases, and through a connecting linkage, vary the incidence of the twin-delta foils below to control their lift and keep them at the required depth.

## Shallow-draft foil system

In the past, this has been employed almost exclusively on commercial and sports hydrofoils designed and built in the Soviet Union. It was developed as a simple, robust system, suitable for use on long, sheltered rivers, lakes, canals and inland seas, and in particular, the many thousands of miles of shallow waterways for which V- or trapeze-foil configurations would be unsuitable because of their relatively deep draft requirements when hullborne. The system, which is also known as the immersion depth-effect system, was evolved by Dr Rostislav Alexeyev. It consists of two main horizontal foils, one forward, one aft, each carrying approximately half the weight of the vessel. A submerged foil loses lift as it approaches the surface from a depth of approximately one chord (the distance between the leading and trailing edges of the foil section). To aid take-off and prevent the vessel from sinking back into the displacement mode, planing subfoils are attached to the forward struts, port and starboard, and are so located that when they are touching the water surface, the main foils are submerged at a depth of approximately one chord.

Since the appearance of the Raketa, the prototype of which was launched in 1957, the Alexeyev system has undergone many modifications in the light of operating experience. Most of the larger designs—the Meteor, Kometa, Sputnik and Vikhr—now incorporate midship stability foils and full width depth-sensor foils forward instead of the earlier stub foils attached to the outer faces of the bow foil struts. A feature of the latest Kometa—the M series—is the employment of a surface-piercing trapeze foil forward with a shallow W pitch-control foil above. The trapeze foil, which is identical to the V-foil apart from the short horizontal section across the base, is inherently stable, the restoring forces being provided by the area of the foil that is submerged.

Alexeyev's shallow-draft submerged foil craft embody charac-teristics of the Grunberg principle of inherent angle of attack variation, substituting planing subfoils for the original displace-ment floats or partly immersed foils. The system comprises a 'wing' foil, split into two in the case of the Raketa, and a stabiliser foil system. The lift of the stabiliser is considerably more respon-sive to draught change than the corresponding 'wing' foil curve. As operational conditions such as centre of gravity travel, fuel, or payload weight and speed change, the 'wing' foil sinks or rises relative to the stabiliser thereby adjusting to demand the angle of attack. The design is such that the 'wing' foil remains adequately submerged at all times during flight and the hull remains at the required height above the mean water level. Each time the sub-foils come into play, and the main foils abandon the narrow limits of the surface-effect zone, the Alexeyev principle becomes inoperative and the Grunberg system automatically takes over.

## Ladder foil

The ladder foil, the earliest form of surface-piercing foil, is exactly like a ladder insofar as it consists of a number of foils set at right angles to their supporting struts. Early ladder foil systems, as used by Forlanini, for example, comprised a single set of ladder foils beneath the hull forward and another set aft. It was soon discovered that this arrangement lacked lateral stability, a disadvantage that was rectified in later craft by the use of two sets of bow foils, one each side of the hull on stub wings, struts or sponsons.

Generally, the foils were flat but occasionally they had a V configuration, the provision of dihedral preventing a sudden change in lift as the foils broke the surface. One of the few craft employing ladder foils today is the Williwaw (Pages 78/79), a 1.6-ton, 30-knot sailing hydrofoil which completed a 16-day passage between Sausalito, California and Kahului Harbour, Maui, Hawaii, in September 1970—the first ocean crossing by a hydrofoil sailboat. Its lateral foils are of four-rung ladder type while the stern foil/rudder is of three-rung ladder configuration. Like the V-foil, the ladder foil is inherently stable, in that its lift varies in relation to flying height or the depth of foil submergence.

## Foil configuration

After an examination of the major differences in foil systems, there is still one further important aspect to study—the distribution of lifting surface area, resulting in the foil being arranged in aeroplane, canard or tandem configurations. In the aeroplane or conventional foil arrangement, the major part of the load is borne by a large single or split foil forward amidships, and a small, lightly loaded foil aft. The opposite to this is the canard system, in which the major portion of the load is borne on a single large main foil or split foil located aft of amidships, and a smaller, lightly-loaded foil at the bow. A tandem foil configuration is one in which the load is shared equally by the bow and stern foil systems.

The most frequent reason for 'splitting' the main foils is to facilitate their retraction sideways out of the water, as on the Boeing Tucumcari, and Grumman Plainview. However, the need for dividing the main foil can be overcome, on a canard foil craft for example, by swinging back the complete mainfoil to a point at the rear of the transom, two examples being the PHM-1 and the Jetfoil. Alternatively, the main foil struts can be retracted vertically into the hull as on the Boeing PCH-1 High Point.

## Cavitation

The occurrence of cavitation is by far the biggest obstacle in the path of those designing water craft capable of achieving high sustained speeds. It is caused at high speed, generally between 40–45 knots, by the pressure drop at a point on the upper surface of a foil or at the back of a propeller, and falls into two categories—stable and unstable. Unstable cavities or vapour bubbles form just behind the foils leading edge and extend across the foil profile and downstream, expanding and collapsing at high frequency. At the point of collapse, pressure peaks reach 20,000 psi. The phenomenon produces severe erosion, and an unstable flow over the foils resulting in abrupt changes in lift and therefore discomfort to passengers.

Most current commercial and military hydrofoils have sub-cavitating foils of NACA section, which provide an even pressure distribution over the entire chord length to provide maximum lift within their cavitation speed limits. To delay the onset of cavitation, relatively low foil loadings of between 1,200–1,400 psf are necessary but there is always some danger of cavitation when operating at speeds of 40–50 knots. Above this speed—at between 45–60 knots—a well-designed and fabricated foil system can cope with the phenomenon for a relatively short duration. But at speeds above 60 knots, special supercavitating foils are necessary. One answer lies in the use of air-stabilised foils, described earlier, but several other approaches are being investigated including transcavitating foils, base-ventilated foils, and various other foil profiles designed to operate efficiently at high speeds while fully cavitated.

The transcavitating foil is of delta shape, and by loading the tip more highly than the root, cavitation is first induced at the foil's tip, then extends spanwise to the foil's root as speed increases. Base ventilation is a system in which air is fed continuously to the upper surface of a wedge-shaped foil, unwetting the surface and preventing the formation of critical areas of decreased pressure. Alternatively, the air may be fed into the cavity formed behind a square trailing edge for drag reduction. This type of foil is also known as a superventilated foil, and has been tested at speeds up to 80 knots in calm waters on the high-speed test craft Fresh-1. The standard wedge-shaped supercavitating section induces from the onset a cavity which covers the entire upper surface and then collapses downstream, well beyond the trailing edge, before collapsing. The lift and drag of these foils is determined by the shape of the leading edge and undersurface.

Research with various types of high-speed foils continues,

especially in the areas of lift generation at take-off, effective lift control, the transition from sub-to-supercavitating speeds and the providing of the thin leading edges with sufficient structural strength.

Another major problem in the design of foil assemblies is air which enters from the free atmosphere and relieves the low pressures created by the water flowing across the foil's upper surface. Air entry, or ventilation as it is sometimes known, occurs particularly when the foil struts are subjected to high angles of attack, during high-speed turns for example. It can also occur through internal passages in the struts. One method of overcoming external air entry is by the use of 'fences', small aerofoil-shaped partitions placed at short intervals along the upper and lower foil surfaces. These are attached on both struts and foils in the direction of the flow, to prevent air ventilation passing down to destroy lift.

## Propulsion

The great majority of commercial hydrofoils today are powered by high-speed diesel engines, which are still the most economical and reliable powerplants for small marine vehicles. As mentioned earlier the advantages of the diesel-powered craft at present are that their purchase cost, fuel and maintenance overheads are lower, and skilled diesel engineers are more readily available for their repair and overhaul. Considering that the light-weight diesel can attain 8–12,000 operating hours between overhauls, the maintenance cost is less than half that of a comparable marinised gas-turbine. Another major consideration is that although the specific weight of a turbine may be only 75–80 per cent. of that of a diesel of the same output, by the time fuel weight is added, the difference in the overall weight fraction for a small vessel is reduced to only 7–10 per cent. in favour of the gas-turbine.

However, the range of available lightweight diesels is limited to an upper limit of 4,000 hp, and so for larger vessels, the employment of gas-turbines becomes essential. In addition, for hydrofoils or larger tonnage, the more powerful gas-turbines do offer substantial advantages. They develop more power per unit of space and weight, are easier to produce, provide very high torque at low rotational speeds, warm-up and accelerate more rapidly and finally, they are available in a selection of powers in combination of one to four engines from 1,000–80,000 hp.

The gas-turbines, like those employed for air-cushion vehicles, are existing aircraft power plants (that for the PHM is developed from the General Electric TF39 which powers the C-5A transport and the DC-10 Trijet), combined with specially designed free-power turbines which convert the gas energy to rotative, mechanical power. The rotor of the turbine is free to rotate independently of the gas generator's speed and can therefore supply variable horse-power output and rotational speeds. Since the gas-turbines were not designed for service in a marine environment, the turbine blades are coated against salt water ingestion and magnesium parts have been replaced with metals with a superior resistance to salt water corrosion.

## Transmission

The simplest forms of transmitting power to the propeller is by inclined shaft or the V-drive, both of which are suitable for small surface-piercing foil and shallow-draft submerged foil craft with keels only a limited height above the mean water level. However, the inclination of the propeller shaft is restricted to about 12–14 degrees to the horizontal (Page 83) to avoid cavitation of the propeller blades. This means that only a limited hull clearance is possible for typically sized craft and the only form of mechanical transmission available which provides the necessary clearance height in high sea-states, is the double right-angle bevel gear or Z-drive. Because of its relative simplicity, the waterjet is now becoming increasingly popular, but at speeds in the range of 35–50 knots, it is less efficient than water propellers. Its use is dictated by its ease of operation, greater reliability and less mechanically complex power transmission. The waterjet system employed on the Boeing Jetfoil is seen on page 83. In this particular installation, power is supplied by two Allison gas-turbines, each of which is connected to an axial-flow water pump through a gearbox. When foilborne, water enters through a duct inlet located at the lower end of the central aft foil strut. At the top of the duct the water is split into two paths and enters into each of the axial flow pumps. It is then discharged at high pressure through nozzles at the base of the transom.

The water flow path in the Jetfoil is the same during hullborne operation as with the foils extended. However, with foils retracted, intake water enters through a flush inlet in the keel. Reversing and steering during hullborne operations, are accomplished by 'buckets' immediately aft of the water exist nozzle which, deflect or reverse the flow.

Waterjet-propelled hydrofoils operating in the 45–60 knot speed range are likely to be seen in great numbers in the future. However, as a thrust producer, the waterjet does not begin to compare with the efficiency of the supercavitating propeller until it is in the speed regime of 80–120 knots. But before this performance can be achieved, a number of hydrodynamic problems must be resolved, and no doubt, research on SES waterjets will help to find some of the solutions.

# CHAPTER THREE

# FERRIES, FRIGATES AND FUNCRAFT

For Frederick Elbe, a Munich economist, 16 August 1974 was the last day of a car journey to the British Isles, where he and his family would spend their summer vacation. He steered his Ford saloon through the centre of Calais, past the docks, then followed the road leading out through the dunes to the International Hoverport. Within minutes the car had drawn up to the main entrance to the building and he switched off the ignition. Suddenly, as if by magic, pretty hostesses, uniformed officials, civic dignitaries, reporters and photographers seemed to converge on him from all directions. Champagne corks popped, glasses were filled and cameras flashed. In next to no time, Herr Elbe and his family were being overwhelmed with gifts and congratulations. Then a banner was produced which explained all! The Elbe's Ford was the 500,000th car to be carried by Hoverlloyd's SR.N4s on the Ramsgate–Calais route since the service started in April 1969. It was a major occasion for two reasons. It marked a further commercial success for Hoverlloyd, but it also meant that yet another milestone had been left behind in man's effort to defeat the water barrier.

Today, the cross-Channel SR.N4s—the 'jumbos' of today's commercial hovercraft—are no longer regarded as an Emett-inspired novelty, designed to lure Continental day trippers into shopping sprees. The craft are accepted throughout Europe by travellers on business or pleasure bound, who judge and compare the services entirely on their merits of speed, cost and comfort. That one person in three prefers to travel by hovercraft, rather than by conventional ferries, is a striking tribute to the untiring efforts of British Hovercraft Corporation, who built the SR.N4s, and the two operators, British Rail Hovercraft (trading as 'Seaspeed') and Hoverlloyd Ltd, who within a decade turned an inventor's dream into dramatic reality.

By March 1975, the three craft operated by Hoverlloyd and the two in service with British Rail Seaspeed, had accumulated between them a total of 6,990,000 passengers and 1,058,000 cars in 52,936 crossings. Profits are now being achieved and expansion of the two fleets is being planned. The two companies carry about 30 per cent. of the total traffic crossing the Straits of Dover annually, even though the five craft represent only 3 per cent. or less of the total displacement tonnage of ship ferries employed on the English Channel routes.

The five craft operate up to 12 hours a day each in all weathers throughout the year. Gale force headwinds and seas in excess of 12 ft occasionally delay services, but it is rare for operations to be suspended for a complete day. Hoverlloyd has attained up to 98 per cent. reliability over long periods, including the peak summer months of July, August and September, when as many as fourteen flights may be made by each craft daily.

Weather is the major hazard, but the operating crews face another potential hazard too. The English Channel is the world's busiest sea lane, with at least 700 ships passing through it at any given time of the day or night. Navigation of the N4s, which cut right across the main traffic streams, clearly demands the exercising of considerable care and skill on the part of the captains and navigators, especially in poor visibility. To help to ensure that no mishaps take place, each craft is equipped with electronic navigation and collision avoidance radar aids. Should a dangerous situation develop, the lift fans can be cut immediately the pitch of the propellers are reversed for maximum braking effect and the craft lowered on to its hull and brought to a standstill in 175 yards.

In the craft's control cabin is a Decca Navigator and Log, a Decca TM 629 main radar and true motion display and a Decca 202 standard radar plus a doppler speed meter. The Flight Log, apart from providing the captain with a continuous fix on a moving map, so that he can maintain the most economical route, can also be used to ensure that N4s with reciprocal headings (and closing speeds in calm water conditions as high as 150 knots) are kept a safe distance apart. The two collision radars are often used in conjunction. By setting the main radar to a 10-mile range the navigator can ensure that all the major obstacles are avoided, while the standby system, set to $\frac{3}{4}$-mile range, enables him to pick out not only very small craft, but also individual fishermen, buoys, shallows, sandbanks and rougher water lying ahead. This enables the captain to take any avoiding action and to reduce speed when necessary to maintain passenger comfort.

The Goodwin Sands, once a dreaded English Channel navigational hazard, which has claimed hundreds of ships over the years, presents no problems to the amphibious SR.N4. Passengers may sense a slight bump as the craft makes the transition from water to the vast banks of sand, which are exposed only at low tide, and again when it returns to skim across the constantly undulating sea.

British Rail Seaspeed launched its cross-Channel service for passengers and cars between the hoverports at Dover and Boulogne in August 1968 with the SR.N4 'Princess Margaret'. A year later the service was augmented by the introduction of a similar craft, 'Princess Anne', and in October 1970, a service was initiated between Dover and Calais. In association with French Railways, a through London–Paris service is operated, taking about six hours. Fast 'Autotrains' operate straight to Paris from a platform alongside the Boulogne hoverport. At Calais the service links with special fast coach connexions with Ostend, Brussels and Lille.

Plans are now advanced to 'stretch' the two Seaspeed SR.N4s to the new Mk III configuration. Each craft will be lengthened by nearly 50 ft, increasing the passenger capacity from 254 to 396 and the vehicle capacity from 30 to 53. The four Marine Proteus gas-turbines are expected to be up-rated to 3,800 shp and each will drive a propeller/fan unit with a larger 21 ft (6.4 m.) diameter propeller. The additional power will ensure that the performance of the earlier SR.N4s will be matched despite the increase in all-up weight from 190 to 265 tons.

In turn, the Mk III will provide much of the operational data needed for the 'new generation' BH.88, which though designed to carry a similar payload, will be very much cheaper to operate. Among its design refinements will be the installation of more economical gas-turbines, the introduction of more efficient lift and propulsion systems, an improved skirt and a new hull to reduce hydrodynamic resistance. BHC predicts that not only will the BH.88 be five knots faster than the SR.N4, but it will also show a 60 per cent. saving in fuel. In fact the fuel used by the BH.88 will be about 2.0 lb/payload per ton-mile, some 15 per cent. less than orthodox ships per unit of payload, a figure which has attracted the attention of car and passenger ferry operators around the world.

Hoverlloyd was formed by two shipping companies, Swedish Lloyd and Swedish American to operate a cross-Channel passenger/car hovercraft ferry service between Ramsgate and Calais and began SR.N4 services in April 1969. The crossing takes 40 minutes and there are up to twenty-one return trips a day in summer and a minimum of four a day in winter. In May 1969 the company opened a coach/hovercraft/coach service between London and Paris. In April 1974 a similar service was opened to Brussels.

All three of Hoverlloyd's SR.N4s have been modified to MkII standard, increasing the capacity of the craft from 254 passengers and 30 vehicles to 280 passengers and 37 vehicles. This modification was achieved by the removal of the two inner passenger cabins on the deck level to accommodate more vehicles. Passenger capacity has been increased by widening the outer cabins to the edge of the craft's raft structure. At a maximum gross weight of 200 tons, the SR.N4 Mk II is far heavier than the Mk I, but the effect of the increase in weight on performance is described as being 'minimal'.

It was partly the success of the SR.N4s that led to the inception of the first EEC hovercraft study, which called for a 2,000-ton vessel capable of providing fast ferry services between the main European and Mediterranean ports. The project, which was basically a detailed technical and economic cooperation proposal, has been temporarily 'shelved' while awaiting an overall assessment of the EEC's transportation requirements. A point of interest is that no fewer than nineteen European and Mediterranean countries asked if they could participate in the planning, construction and operation of these ship-size hovercraft.

Matching the size of the SR.N4s, is a new French craft, the SEDAM Naviplane N 500, a 240 tonne mixed traffic ferry with a top speed of 76 knots. Instead of accommodating both cars and passengers on the same deck, the N 500 has a twin-deck layout, with passengers accommodated on the upper deck and vehicles on the lower. The basic model is designed for 400 passengers and 45 cars.

A possible contender from North America in the 200-ton-plus bracket is the Bell Vanguard, a projected mixed-traffic ferry based on the Jeff (B) assault landing craft configuration, but with twice the length and beam. The craft will be capable of carrying fifty-four large cars and 192 passengers. The cars will be carried on the open central deck, while the passengers will be accommodated in cabins in port and starboard sidestructures. Amongst the routes for which the craft is thought to be suitable are Portland, Maine—Yarmouth, Nova Scotia, Victoria Island—Vancouver BC and on Prince Edward Island.

The next largest commercial craft, in commercial use is the 50-ton Mitsui MV-PP15. The company, which is a BHC and HDL licencee, has built three of these 155-seat hoverferries which are powered by two Avco Lycoming TF 25 gas-turbines and can cruise at about 50 knots. Visually speaking, the craft is a scaled-up version of the Mitsui MV-PP5, a 50-seater. Twelve of these craft are successfully operating a number of fast-ferry services in Japanese coastal and inland waters. A feature of the MV-PP15 and MV-PP5 is the use of two retractable wheels, located aft, which can be extended downwards into the water to prevent drift when turning and assist braking at high speeds. On land, the wheels assist manoeuvring and help to reduce skirt wear.

In Canada, Bell has started the production of the 40-ton Voyageur and the 17-ton Viking, two rugged flat-deck trans-porters specially designed to face the rigours of the Arctic. The basic Voyageur is a twin-engined, fully amphibious machine, able to haul payloads of up to 25 tons at speeds up to 54 mph. Since its payload is equal to that of most heavy transport aircraft engaged in regular supply operations in the North, it can provide a direct transport link from airstrips to settlements and support bases for the movement of men, equipment and supplies. By adding superstructures to the flat deck, the craft can be used for various alternative roles from a 140-seat 'bus' to a military weapons platform.

One of the first operators of the Voyageur (Pages 32 and 33) is the Canadian Coast Guard Hovercraft Unit, which has been patrolling the Straits of Georgia and the Gulf Islands—an area of about 500 square miles—with an SR.N5 since April 1969. The unit has undertaken well over 400 search and rescue missions, directly involving nearly 500 people during aircraft, marine and other emergencies. Other operations for which the unit's hover-craft are employed are the checking and servicing of marine navigational aids, aircraft accident investigation, water pollution investigation, the carriage of steamship inspectors for on-the-spot safety checks of tugs, working with police departments, exercises with the Royal Canadian Navy, government experimental work, and the training and familiarisation of government personnel with hovercraft.

One unexpected application of the CCG's Voyageur during its trials programme was that of icebreaker. The trials, undertaken in early 1974, were made to compare the icebreaking capability of the self-propelled Voyageur against that of the non-self-propelled ACT-100, ACV transporter.

Eventually it was established that there are two methods of breaking ice using air cushion technology, high speed and slow speed. At high speed the critical velocity depends on the ice thickness, its flexural strength and the water depth. The Voyageur was operated at about 12–15 mph back and forth across the ice setting up standing waves, half a craft length astern, similar to the waves created by displacement craft in water. The ice broke up at the crest of the waves. It was found that the Voyageur could break up hard ice up to 15 inches thick continuously, leaving a trail of broken ice about 120 ft wide.

Visual observation and special cameras mounted under the skirts revealed what happens when an ACV approaches an ice sheet at slow speeds and how the ice-breaking phenomenon takes place. Once contact has been made with the ice sheet, the skirt rises above the ice while continuing to form an effective air seal. The ice sheet soon arrives in the main zone of pressurised air beneath the craft where the water level is depressed to a lower level than the bottom of the ice layer. The ice now lacks the support of the water beneath and when it reaches its critical length, the overhanging section breaks off and falls into the water beneath.

Within months, the discovery had been put to excellent practical use. Engineers at Arctic Engineers and Constructors, builders of the 250-ton ACT-100, the first vehicle to display the ice-breaking potential of the ACV, sat down and designed the VIBAC (Vehicle, Ice-Breaking, Air Cushion) system, an air-cushion applicator designed specifically to aid the passage of a conventional ship through ice-bound waters. The vehicle is locked on to the bow of the ship as soon as it approaches the ice-field. A plough-like deflector beneath thrusts aside the broken ice as the vessel makes its way through the ice sheet (Page 65).

Both Canada and Alaska are likely to become important ACV 'breeding' grounds as such craft appear to be the only means of providing transport in Arctic regions economically. Water transport in the Canadian Arctic can only be used for about three months during the summer, and the ACV is seen as the only vehicle likely to assist in the rapid development of these regions. In addition to the exceptionally short shipping season of the North Slope further stimulus to the employment of ACVs in Alaska is the government decision to restrict the movement of conventional vehicles to prepared surfaces only. The reason for this is that during the short Arctic summer, the few feet of ground above the permafrost (the frozen Arctic subsoil), thaws and turns into a bog. In their attempt to negotiate the wet mass of soil and vegetation in main centres of activity, wheeled and track vehicles may cause long-lasting ruts which do irreparable damage to the surface ecology and there is danger that the balance may be disturbed.

One medium-size ferry which is giving excellent service in France is SEDAM's Naviplane N 300, the company's first full-scale vehicle designed for commercial use. The craft is operated by the Bordeaux Port Authority on a passenger/car ferry service across the Gironde estuary, between Blaye and Lamarque, carrying up to four cars and thirty-eight passengers per crossing. It operates thirty crossings per day, seven days a week and has maintained an exceptional record for reliability over the past few years. A production model is under development and construction is being planned.

Probably the best known hovercraft of all is BHC's SR.N6 Winchester, variants of which have been employed since 1967 on trials, sales demonstrations and operations in Africa, Canada, Denmark, Finland, India, South America and the Middle and Far East, logging nearly 200,000 operating hours. Commercial variants of the Winchester and the earlier SR.N5 Warden are now in service with British Rail Hovercraft Ltd; the Department of Civil Aviation in New Zealand; Department of Transport, Canada; Hovertravel Ltd; Hoverwork Ltd, and Mitsubishi Heavy Industries Ltd. Many others are in service with military and paramilitary organisations throughout the world.

Development of the Winchester Class continues, with the latest Mk 6 variants offering additional payload, improved all-weather performance and a substantial reduction in propeller noise. Available in an increasing variety of configurations, the new models feature a more powerful engine, twin-propellers, a redesigned skirt and an increase of 10 ft (3.04 m.) in overall length. The pitch of each propeller can be varied independently, giving the captain greatly improved directional control at high and low speeds. Earlier models relied on aerodynamic rudders for directional control, and at low speeds, the use of thrust or 'puff' ports in the cushion-supply ducting.

The SR.N6, in the hands of leading operators like Hoverwork Ltd, has probably played a greater part in gaining world wide acceptance for the air-cushion vehicle than any other single factor. Hovercwork Ltd, a sister company to Hovertravel Ltd, whose main activity is the operation of two SR.N6 passenger ferries across the Solent between Ryde and Southsea, is devoted largely to charter work. It has provided N6s for film sequences, crew training, and mineral surveys. Since 1966, its craft, which include a 5-ton flat-deck version of the N6 and a similarly converted SR.N5, has supported surveys in fourteen different countries, representing almost every climatic condition from Arctic cold to equatorial heat. It also operated the hovercraft passenger service for Expo' 67 at Montreal, and a service at the 1970 Algiers Exposition. Between them, Hovertravel and Hover-work, represent the most experienced profit-making ACV operation in the world. They employ a staff of about fifty, including twelve captains and eighteen maintenance engineers.

Another well-known passenger/utility ACV is the Hovermarine HM 2, some forty of which were in service or on order at the time of writing. The craft, which contains its air cushion between rigid sidewalls and flexible skirts fore and aft, is powered by three diesel engines. The fast ferry model carries 62–65 passengers or 5 tons of freight at speeds up to 35 knots. The general purpose model is suited to a variety of roles from custom and police patrol to search and rescue duties and hydrographic survey. In the latter role, the HM 2 is equipped with a Decca navigation equipment, an autopilot, echo-sounding gear and a computer. The system has been described as a 'hydrographer's dream' since it is fully automated and allows a four-man crew to undertake pre-programmed surveys of coastal and harbour waters at high speed without manual control.

The vessel operates at about 35 knots, about three times as fast as conventional survey ships, and offers the additional advantage of having a hovering draft of less than 3 ft. This means that the hydrographer can survey rivers, lagoons and estuaries where restricted draft conditions are too hazardous for normal displace-ment craft. Surveys undertaken with the HM.2 are performed automatically after feeding the required track to the Omnitrac computer. The autopilot is linked either to the compass, so that it steers a selected automatic course, or to the Omnitrac computer, which obtains position-fixing signals via a receiver from a Decca main or survey chain. Depth and positional data are recorded on punched tape as the craft follows the desired survey lines and the data collected is processed ashore in final chart form.

Production of HM.2s for North and Central America is being

undertaken by Hovermarine's factory at Titusville, Florida, whilst the company's UK subsidiary in Southampton builds craft for the rest of the world. Larger derivatives of the HM.2 are being planned, one recently announced model being the 140–200 seat HM.5. The only other commercial sidewall craft either in production or intended for production today are the Zarnitsa, a waterjet-propelled, 48–50 seater being built in the Soviet Union, and two larger derivatives, the Rassvet and Orion, both of which seat eighty passengers. The former is designed for offshore work and the latter for services on both secondary and major rivers, estuaries, lakes and reservoirs.

The world of ACVs is by no means limited to craft designed for scheduled passenger services and the carriage of freight. Hundreds of smaller vehicles are in use for scores of utility applications for which other types of transport are either totally unsuitable or far too expensive. Others are built and driven just for sheer pleasure and the stimulation of being able to cross land, water, marshland, mud, snow and ice at high speed without fear of either sinking or being bogged down.

Almost anywhere in the world with a high dependence on water transport is a potential market for the light-to-medium weight ACV. British-designed lightweight machines like the Cushioncraft CC-7, variants of the inflatable-hulled Pindair Skima, the Sealand Hovercraft SH-2, Air Bearings' AB11 Crossbow and a number of others are selling in increasing numbers to areas where there is a steady demand for small fast vessels with amphibious capability. Users of the Skima 4, for example, include missionaries on Lake Chad, an aluminium company in the Arabian Gulf, a pest research organisation, a marine biology research group, subaqua organisations, exploration groups and flood relief and beach rescue organisations.

In Australia, where a number of promising light ACVs have been built, two Taylorcraft Skimaire 1s are operated by the Mudginberri Station Pty Ltd. The general manager, Leith Andrews, believes these fibre-glass-hulled three-seaters are the only ACVs in the world to be used to round-up livestock. The craft are operated across the station's swamps and mud flats to muster buffalo which are then slaughtered and dressed ready for export. Elsewhere in Australia, at the Coorong National Park, the National Parks Commission employs a Taylorcraft Skimaire to prevent the illegal poaching of water fowl on the 90-mile long Coorong Lake, which connects with the Murray River and the sea.

Even smaller than the Skimaire and its contemporaries are the hundreds of ultra-light craft built by individuals for racing or simply as runabouts. Interest in the construction and safe operation of these craft is fostered by the Hover Club of Great Britain Ltd, which provides technical advice to amateur builders and each year organises race meetings and other events. Although established mainly for light ACV enthusiasts in the United Kingdom, it has many overseas members and keeps them up-to-date with its activities and light hovercraft developments through a monthly news letter.

Apart from helping to evoke public interest in hovercraft, amateur machines frequently introduce new ideas in thrust, lift, skirt or control systems, some of which may be used to improve the performance of full-size hovercraft. Conversely, the designers of larger machines can approach the amateur to test a scaled-down design modification on a small, racing machine, before incorporating it on a large craft. The use of manned or un-manned radio-controlled dynamic models for research is a practice employed throughout the industry.

## Military hovercraft (Surface Effect Vehicles)

In view of their higher speed, compact design and reduced crew requirements, ACVs are also in increasing demand for defence purposes. An additional attraction is that the smaller, multi-terrain craft can operate totally independently of deep water ports, drydocks and other expensive facilities which for many years have been considered a prerequisite of a strong naval defence system. A squadron of missile-equipped hovercraft can face an equal number of conventional warships with impunity. In terms of first cost, maintenance, fuelling, crewing and shore facilities, the hovercraft squadron would be only a fraction of the price of the conventional craft.

Hovercraft like the BH.7 Wellington (Pages 24 and 27) have already led to the development of a completely new coastal defence system which dispenses entirely with the time-honoured concept of standing off-shore patrols. Operating in conjunction with early warning surveillance radar, in much the same way as jet fighters, they are 'scrambled' to intercept and interrogate suspect craft by a sector controller. Alternatively, they can be controlled from a mobile base, like a 'mother' ship patrolling off-shore. While on stand-by, the craft are deployed either on hardstandings above the shoreline or dispersed amid dunes for concealment. In the Persian Gulf, the Imperial Iranian Navy currently employs a squadron of eight SR.N6 Winchesters and four BH.7s, with two more on order. Their duties include the security of oil traffic, the control of smuggling, support of isolated police posts and counter-insurgency operations.

In what has been described as the first tactical employment of ACVs since the US Army and Navy's SK-5s left Vietnam, hovercraft units of the IIN, using SR.N6s and BH.7s occupied three strategic islands in the Persian Gulf in 1969, to ensure Iranian command of the Straits of Hormez. Another Middle Eastern country operating SR.N6s is Saudi Arabia, which has a squadron of eight craft based at Jedda and Aziziyah. The Saudi Arabian Coastal and Frontier Force uses the craft for contraband control, search and rescue and liaison duties.

Just how effective a craft like the SR.N6 can be when employed on contraband control was demonstrated in 1969, when one was chartered by the Indian Ministry of Finance to intercept gold smugglers operating to India in fast motorised dhows from the Arabian coast. Within a relatively few weeks about 300 interceptions were made, mainly at night, and in one, gold worth about £200,000 was seized by customs men who accompanied the sorties. The operation proved so effective that for a long period the smuggling stopped.

At the time of writing, it was estimated that nearly seventy nations are either operating ACVs, ordering them, or seeking quotations for craft ranging from air-dropped inflatable four-seaters to 4,000-ton freighters.

Two major companies in the United States are hard at work on an interim programme which will enable the US Navy to build a very much bigger craft of 2,200 tons. The projected 2,200 ton, combat-capable test craft would be twice the size and have eleven times the displacement of the 200-ton SR.N4, the largest hovercraft in service today. If the new programmes, which are being conducted by Bell Aerospace and Rohr Industries, are successful an order for a prototype is expected to be placed by June 1976.

The 2,200 ton ship will be powered by General Electric LM-2500 gas-turbines driving waterjets and its top speed is expected to be 80–100 knots. One of the reasons why the US Navy is anxious to have a 2,200 ton vehicle available for tests as soon as possible is that this is the smallest size craft suitable for testing on the open ocean, and until a vessel of this size is available it will be difficult to determine the feasibility of 5,000–10,000 ton ships. Should the prototype prove successful, one of the US Navy's initial aims is the laying down of a new class of warship in the 2–3,000-ton range for use as escorts, ASW helicopter and VSTOL platforms and as missile-armed surface combatants.

At the same time projects for very much larger SESs of 6,000–10,000 tons are being assessed with a view to their use as sea-control ships and high-value cargo carriers. Impetus to the US Navy's ACV programme was given by Admiral Elmo Zumwalt, the US Navy's dynamic ex-Chief of Naval Operations, who saw in SESs, the opportunity to lay the foundations of the world's first 100-knot navy. He set a very high priority on the concept in the belief that it offered for the first time since World War II, a chance for destroyer-size ASW vessels to regain a decided speed advantage over submerged submarines, now averaging speeds of 30–35 knots, or being roughly three times faster than their 1939–45 predecessors.

It was also felt that if the US Navy could introduce SESs in sufficient numbers soon enough, its loss of naval superiority could be redressed. Surface-effect warships carrying ship-to-ship missiles, helicopters or V/STOL attack aircraft like the Harrier, would have a substantial tactical advantage over the fastest displacement ships and equipped with the type of ASW sustained detection equipment and weapons carried aboard the latest frigates, they would also prove ideal for countering the potentially critical submarine menace. Apart from its high speed, the SES has minimal water contact, provides a low noise signature and is a difficult target for torpedoes. Employed as an aircraft carrier, its speed would reduce the relative speed of approach of conventional aircraft, simplifying landings. As a logistics transport, the SES could complete the trans-Atlantic crossing in 30 hours with multi-thousand-ton payloads, permitting the US armed services to reduce the number of personnel based overseas, without compromising the ability to respond immediately in an emergency.

One 600-ton SEV in the design stage at Boeing is intended to meet the anticipated needs of the US services in the Arctic. This huge wasteland of ice and tundra is one of man's most hostile environments, but at the same time it is an area of vital strategic importance in terms of guarding the northern approaches to the USA and Canada. The object of the design, completed under the Arctic Surface Effect Vehicle Programme—a project conducted by the Advanced Research Projects Agency of the Department of Defence—is to demonstrate the potential of the SEV as an all-weather, high performance, long-range military platform.

In Europe, the potential of the seagoing ACV warship has led to extensive studies being conducted by the French navy, whose immediate aim is to develop an ASW frigate of 2–4,000 tons. Another major power expressing interest in this new approach to seapower is the Soviet Union, which is already operating an experimental, armed logistics craft similar in size and shape to the SR.N4, and starting to build larger craft.

In the United Kingdom one of the latest military ACVs is the 100-ton Vosper Thornycroft VT 2, which began trials in the summer of 1975. It is the first fully-amphibious craft to be built by the company and employs air propulsion instead of the water propellers used on its precedessor, the VT 1.

Naval planners have no doubt that the SES will revolutionise naval strategy in the years to come. Some go so far as to suggest that by the mid-1980s, today's warships will have become museum pieces.

# CHAPTER FOUR

# SHIPS THAT FLY

Despite the undoubted success of the Supramar PT 10 Freccia d'Ore on Lake Maggiore in 1953, the great majority of shipping companies argued fiercely against the idea of introducing hydrofoils on their own ferry services. It took von Schertel and the indefatigable Rodriquez five years of sales tours, lectures and route presentations before shipowners began to forget their deep-rooted prejudices against 'novel craft'.

Between 1953 and 1957, only five vessels of Supramar design were put into passenger service. Then suddenly in 1958, the shipping industry, after a penetrating assessment of the whole hydrofoil concept, decided to accept it. By the end of the year, nearly a score of vessels were either being built or had been ordered for operators in Argentina, Italy, Sweden, Finland, Norway, Switzerland and Venezuela. From then until the present day, vessels based on the Schertel–Sachsenberg V-foil system have been in continuous production with, today, three licensed yards—Hitachi, Supramar Pacific Shipbuilding and Vosper Thornycroft Private Ltd—each building vessels at a rate of upwards of six a year.

## Speed and luxury

Representing a complete breakaway from the traditional passenger ferry, the hydrofoils proved an instant success wherever they were introduced. Their graceful flowing lines and aluminium construction were at once more identifiable with the bustling efficiency of the jet-age than the slow pace of the familiar water-bus scene. Not only were they fast, they were far more comfortable and encouraged greater sophistication in passenger handling. Smartly dressed hostesses welcomed passengers aboard and showed them to their saloons, many of which had bars, where light snacks and drinks could be purchased.

Sitting back in their adjustable, airliner-style seats, the passengers were greeted by the captain and given details of the flight. Within a minute or two they had left the jetty or pontoon and before realising it had become foilborne. They were now 'flying' towards their destination at 35 knots—three times faster than any of the conventional craft on the waterway. The journey was completely smooth, apart from a bump or two when hitting the wake of large, passing tankers or striking driftwood. On rare occasions, floating debris would catch on a foil or strut, in which case it would be cleared in minutes by stopping and reversing.

Commuters, shoppers, tourists and those who simply wanted to do something different, all queued to try out the new 'flying boats'. Fares were found to be comparable to railway fares and commuters would purchase weekly, monthly or annual season tickets or carnets similar to those issued on the Paris 'Metro'. Special concession rates were more often than not available for groups, pensioners, military personnel on leave, students, school-children and infants.

Hydrofoil operators soon discovered that, because of their high cruising speed, the craft were able to compete with fast trains and buses. This was possible, however, only in areas where the distance by water was less than that by the coastal road or rail route, resulting in the landborne vehicle having to make long detours around bays and inlets. In Norway, Italy and Japan, they were found to be capable of competing with aircraft over short distances, because of their low operating costs and ability to operate from point-to-point, cutting out the journeys to and from the airport. Other advantages quickly came to light too. For example, when foilborne, the hydrofoil is totally unaffected by tides and currents which means that the operator has no difficulty in maintaining his schedules. Another factor in its favour, is that the passenger mileage per hour, or the daily distance covered, is increased by the ratio of its speed to that of comparable payload displacement boats. Because hydrofoils develop about three times the speed of conventional craft, their transport capacity is three times greater, which means that one hydrofoil boat can replace three ordinary vessels of the same payload. Their fuel consumption is very low, too. A commercial propeller-driven hydrofoil requires only half the power of a conventional vessel to attain the same speed. As a result, the cruising range is substantially increased.

Soon the combination of speed, passenger appeal and reliability had resulted in phenomenal traffic increases. One of the most prosperous of the pioneer services is that operated by Naveca on the twenty-five mile route between Maracaibo and

Cabimas, in Venezuela. Initially two PT 20s operated the service, carrying between them an average of 1,700 passengers daily, or more than 600,000 annually. Both vessels were amortized by Naveca within the first twelve months, and the number of craft employed on the route was quickly doubled.

Among Europe's best known hydrofoil services, is that operated jointly by the Stavanger and the Sandnaes Steam Ship Companies between Stavanger and Bergen, a distance of about 100 nautical miles. The company took delivery from Rodriquez of its first PT 50, Vingtor, in May 1960, and the experience gained with this vessel during her first season was so encouraging that a sister PT 50, Sleipner, was delivered in the spring of 1961. By operating the two craft it was possible to establish a service with sailings twice daily in each direction.

The Norwegian coastline, though one of the world's most attractive, is largely mountainous and deeply scored with fiords. Roads are poor and the mountains and fiords make it impossible to build straight roads or rail links between north and south. The travel time saved by the use of the hydrofoils is considerable. By PT 50, the journey between Bergen and Stavanger via Haugesund takes $3\frac{1}{2}$ hours, instead of rather more than 10 hours by the conventional steamer. With westerly gales, the conditions, particularly on the stretches open to the North Sea, can be quite rough, but the owners state that even under the most unfavourable conditions, the PT 50s have proved remarkably seaworthy.

Late in 1961, the company introduced the PT 20 Ekspressen into service on a 'local' route linking Stavanger with the main communities in the Ryfylkefjords. The service enables farmers and the industrial population of the area to travel to and from Stavanger quicker than by road or rail.

By the early 1960s, hydrofoils were beginning to appear the world over. In Japan, the Ministry of Transport realised the potential of these craft as a means of relieving the burden of the public transport systems operating between the main coastal cities. Japan has one of the highest population densities in the world, and for many years there had been a tendency for the population to concentrate around new towns and cities built on the coastline. Since the speed of the average ferry boat is so much lower than that of landborne transport, hydrofoils seemed to be an obvious answer, particularly as they would be free of normal hindrances like road traffic jams. Both Hitachi and Mitsubishi

Top: *First commercial hydrofoil was Supramar's PT 10, which opened the world's first hydrofoil ferry service between Locarno and Arono, on Lake Maggiore, on 16 May 1953.*

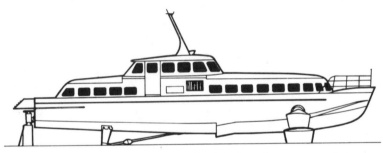

Centre: *The world's first mainland-to-island service was opened by a Supramar PT 20, operating between Messina and Reggio Calabria, in August 1956.*

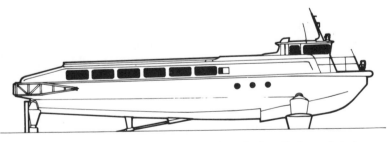

Bottom: *The PL 28 is derived from the PT 27, the first oil-rig supply hydrofoil, three of which have been in service for more than ten years with the Shell Oil Company on Maracaibo Lake, Venezuela.*

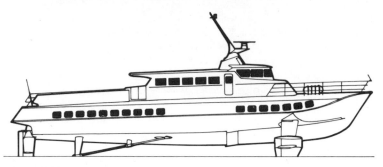

Top: *PT 50, a 63-ton passenger ferry for offshore and inter-island services. Many are now operating regular passenger services in areas ranging from the Mediterranean and Baltic to South America and the Japanese Inland Sea.*

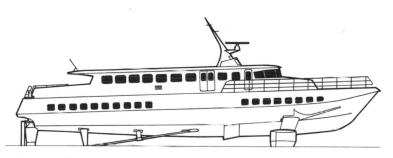

Centre: *Top speed of the 160-seat PTS 75 Mk III is 38.5 knots. Air stabilisation is fitted and the first two vessels of this type are operating between Hong Kong and Macao.*

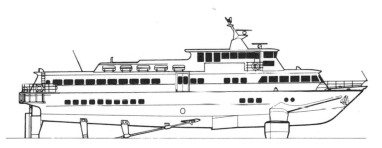

Bottom: *Biggest commercial hydrofoil in service today is the 165-ton Supramar PT 150 Mk III. Three of these 250-seat passenger ferries operate between Malmo and Copenhagen.*

began building hydrofoils, with Hitachi concentrating on Supramar PT 20s and PT 50s, and Mitsubishi on the 80-passenger MH 30. The country now has at least eight operators, with a total of nearly fifty craft between them.

Hitachi-built vessels have been supplied not only to Japanese operators, but also to operators in Hong Kong, Australia and the Philippines. The Hong Kong–Macao route is served by two companies, Far East Hydrofoils Co and Hong Kong–Macao Hydrofoil Co, who between them operate the biggest fleet of hydrofoils outside the Soviet Union—a total of twenty-two craft. In 1967 one of the two companies carried 273,000 passengers. This figure trebled to 839,370 in 1972, with seven craft in operation, and represented a load factor of about 71 per cent. The total number of passengers carried by both companies in 1972 was around 1.8 million. Studies made by Supramar indicate that if the present growth pattern continues, the market potential by 1977 is over seven million passengers, of which rather more than half are expected to travel by hydrofoil. Between them, the vessels either ordered for or operating on the Hong Kong–Macao route represent almost every stage in the development of the commercial hydrofoil over the past twenty years. They include PT 50s, RHS 110s, RHS 140s, RHS 160s, PTS 75s and Boeing Jetfoils.

The Rodriquez RHS series was the outcome of a link established between Rodriquez and the Hamilton Standard Division of United Aircraft Corporation in 1970. This led to the introduction of a range of V-foil craft, which though outwardly similar to the earlier Rodriquez-built vessels, incorporate Hamilton Standard's two-axis seakeeping augmentation systems and have re-styled hulls. The system, similar to that evolved for the FMC Corporation's LVHX-2 amphibious landing craft, is designed to extend the foilborne capabilities of surface-piercing designs in rough seas. It prevents the craft settling in a following sea, provides additional stability in heave and roll, and ensures that it flies through waves higher than the hull clearance height rather than contouring them, thereby reducing vertical motions and accelerations.

Two other important hydrofoil routes are Malmo–Copenhagen, operated by nine craft, and Naples–Capri–Ischia, served by a number of Rodriquez-built PT 20s, PT 50s and Russian-built Kometas. One of the most advanced vessels in service in Scandinavian waters is the Supramar PTS 150 Mk III, three of

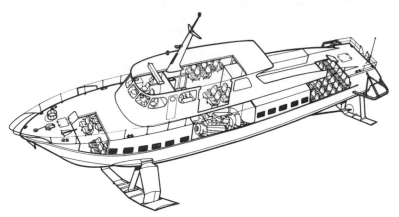

*Interior arrangement of the Rodriquez-built Supramar PT 50/S Caribe. Note the fences on the foils fitted in the direction of the flow, to prevent air filtering down and destroying lift.*

which were built by Westermoen. Biggest seagoing commercial hydrofoil in service today, the PTS 150 seats 250 passengers and is equipped with Schertel–Supramar air stabilisation. Powered by two 3,400 hp MTU marine diesels, it cruises at 36.5 knots and can operate comfortably in head seas in waves 10 ft (3.0 m.) high.

## Safety in operation

Understandably, rigorous attention has been given to safety requirements in hydrofoil ferries since their introduction. In the West, Supramar craft have established the enviable record of having operated over two billion passenger miles since 1953 without causing a single fatality.

Among the basic requirements of any form of high-speed water transportation are a short stopping distance and a small turning radius. Early on, the PT 20 demonstrated that the time elapsing between full speed (34 knots) and dropping on to the hull was between six and seven seconds only, and the total stopping distance was only 230 ft, or a little over three times its length. At cruising speed, its turning radius proved to be about six times the boat length, and its response to rudder deflections was sufficiently fast to avoid striking floating debris and other obstacles. The turning and braking performance has proved to be typical of that of a number of subsequent fixed-foil craft.

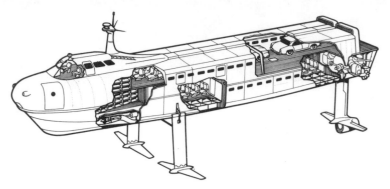

*Cutaway showing features of the mixed passenger/car ferry version of Aéro-spatiales's projected SA 800. Two 1,300 shp Turbomeca 111C gas-turbines will drive the SOGREAH waterjet propulsion unit mounted at the base of the aft foil strut. As a passenger ferry, the craft will carry 200—seats for 116 are provided on the upper deck and 84 on the lower. In mixed-traffic configuration it will carry eight–ten cars on the upper deck, with the lower deck seating eighty-four.*

'Strikes', when they occur, are normally with semi-buoyant items of debris, unobserved from the wheelhouse because they are lying hidden beneath the surface. Should the items of debris —whether discarded railway sleepers (railroad ties), wooden roofing beams or lengths of tree trunk—prove too difficult to remove by reversing, one of the vessel's crew normally dons a wet suit and dives down to loosen or remove the object. In heavily polluted seas and waterways, the debris most commonly encountered is the large plastic bag or plastic sheet, which wraps itself around the leading edge of the bow foil, thus altering the profile and reducing lift.

Normal experience has shown that the momentum of the steel foils is sufficient to chop even the largest sections of wood into pieces. However, to prevent major damage to the hull in the event of the foils being unable to cut through an outsize piece of debris or throw it aside, specially stressed points are provided on most designs between the hull and the foil structure. These allow the front foils to break off, leaving the hull with its passengers intact after the collision.

This system, originated by Supramar, was developed with the aid of model tests in the towing tank at the Research Institute for Shipbuilding in Berlin. Stressed points or 'shear points', as they are more generally known, were built into the struts supporting the bow foil of the model. The shear points were designed to operate at a maximum horizontal hull deceleration of 1 g. Tests showed that the time required to break the forward foil off was only 0.1 of a second, and for passengers sitting in their seats, deceleration of this order was not considered dangerous in any way. The model tests also showed that after a collision and foil separation, the hull always landed on the water horizontally. All commercial hydrofoils have watertight compartments below the passenger decks and in other parts of the main hull, and some are filled with foam-type plastic, making the vessel practically unsinkable.

For regular foil inspection, routine maintenance or the replacement of propellers or drive shafts, the vessels are raised from the water by either floating or quayside cranes, or hoisting with winches. Special hoisting points or bosses are provided on the hulls for this purpose. Metal cradles are normally supplied to support the vessels and their foils when dockside maintenance is being undertaken.

## Hydrofoils in the USA

Attempts to launch and sustain hydrofoil services in the United States have so far met with little success, although there are many hundreds of suitable rivers, inland waterways and off-shore sea routes which offer potential for their operation.

The first hydrofoil to be certified by the US Coast Guard for passenger services was the Honold Albatross, a 28-seat, V-foiled craft designed by Helmut Kock. Twenty-five of these craft were built originally for the New York World's Fair hydrofoil services and afterwards were sold by American Hydrofoils Inc. to other operators. New York's first hydrofoil commuter service was inaugurated with the departure of an Albatross from Port Washington, Long Island, bound for the foot of Wall Street, Manhattan, on 15 July 1963. Albatross operators at one stage included United States Hydrofoils, Miami; New York Hydrofoils Inc., Florida Hydrofoils and Crillon Tours Ltd, La Paz, Bolivia. A number of vessels of the Albatross class are still in service.

One of the best known names in the world of hydrofoils is that of Grumman. Persistent troubles with the original Z-drive system led the company to abandon its otherwise highly successful Blohm & Voss-built Dolphin, one of which was operated in 1969 by Bahamas Hydrolines Ltd between Miami Beach and Freeport,

Grand Bahamas Island. The craft, which carried 50 passengers and a crew of five, completed the 87-mile run in less than two hours. Its cruising speed was 48 knots and, because of its incidence-controlled submerged foils, it was able to maintain schedules in 8–10 ft (2.4–3.0 m.) waves. The prototype Dolphin was completed in 1966. Its speed stood unmatched among commercial hydrofoils until the introduction of the Boeing Jetfoil in Hong Kong and Hawaii in 1975.

The distinction of being the world's first craft with a fully submerged foil system to go into service went to the Atlantic Sea World, a 28-seat, diesel-powered craft, with control flaps operated by the Savitsky system, described in Chapter Two. Four craft of this type have been in continuous service since 1964 with Sea World Inc. of Mission Bay, San Diego, proprietors of the world's biggest oceanarium. The craft carry sightseers over a route of about six miles and are capable of 44 knots. They were the first hydrofoils built on the West Coast to be licensed for commercial use by the US Coast Guard.

Another advanced hydrofoil concept from the USA, now abandoned unfortunately, was the Maryland Victoria, a 75-seat gas-turbine-powered passenger ferry, designed by Gibbs and Cox, and built by Maryland Shipbuilding and Drydock Co. for Northwest Hydrofoil Lines Inc. The prototype, which cruised at 37–40 knots originally operated between Seattle and Victoria BC, and was then taken over by International Hydrolines' Western Division for a service linking San Pedro with Catalina Island, California. According to one report, one of its two LM 100 gas-turbines was badly damaged and not repaired, which led to this otherwise highly successful design being withdrawn from service.

## Hydrofoils in the USSR

Hydrofoils utilise to the utmost the main economic advantage of water transport over other forms of conveyance—its cheapness. Passengers are attracted to them since, unlike displacement craft, they can carry them at speeds equal or comparable to buses and trains with similar or greater comfort. One country which has had absolutely no doubt about the potential of the hydrofoil is the Soviet Union. Experiments began at the Admiralty Shipyards, Leningrad, and at the Sormovo Shipyards at Gorky on the Volga in 1945, only months after the occupation of the Sachsenberg

Shipyard at Dassau Rosslau on the Elbe, where Hanns von Schertel and his team had been building hydrofoils since August 1939.

The discovery of the advanced state of German hydrofoil technology led to the birth of two 'design groups'. The first, at Leningrad, concentrates on the development of V-foil and fully submerged foil craft for both commercial and military use, and the second, at Gorky, led by Dr Rostislav Alexeyev, specialises in shallow draft submerged foils for fast passenger ferry services between the towns and cities along the inland seas, lakes, rivers, canals and reservoirs, from the Soviet Danube in the West to Central Russia and the Far East.

Alexeyev designed and built the Raketa, the very first of the Soviet Union's multi-seat hydrofoil series, a 90-ft single-screw vessel with light, airliner-type seats for sixty-six passengers. The prototype started a trial service between Gorky and Kagan, on the Volga, on 25 August 1957. During the first year of operation, the Raketa carried 10,000 passengers. Ten years later, the single craft had been augmented by scores of other Raketas, Meteors, Kometas and also by experimental craft like the Sputnik, Vikhr and Burevestnik, and the total passengers carried in 1967 had risen to three million. Now in a single season of navigable weather they carry 20 million passengers and this figure is expected to rise every year. The Raketa, now gradually being replaced by the Voskhod, gave excellent service and has extremely low running costs. Claims have been made that the cost of carrying passengers in the Raketa is lower than that of either normal passenger ferries or buses.

Similar low-cost operation is claimed for the 260-passenger Sputnik, employed on the Moscow–Astrakhan service. Early on it was discovered that the cost of operating the Sputnik on the service was 8 per cent. of that of the latest displacement ferry of the United Volga Steamship Line. Many of the vessels operate to communities which, but for the hydrofoils, would have no fast means of communication apart from occasional calls by light aircraft or helicopters. In these areas the rivers have become natural highways and the hydrofoils have taken over the functions of trains and road vehicles. After arrival at a hydrofoil waterbus station, the last leg of a journey is frequently performed in a Volga water-taxi.

Even where alternative landborne methods of transportation exist, hydrofoils frequently deliver their passengers to their

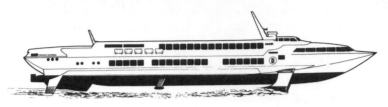

*An enlarged, double-deck derivative of the Soviet Kometa, the Cyclone, is a 250-seater propelled by waterjets. Top speed will be 45–50 knots.*

destinations faster than trains. The Raketa service from Gorky to Kagan, for example, a distance of 516 miles (800 km), takes only 12 hours, while the train takes 20 hours. A conventional passenger ship requires about three days to cover the 559 miles (900 km) from Moscow to Sormovo. The Meteor, another of Alexeyev's designs, covers the distance in just under 14 hours.

Besides the many hundreds of craft on inland waterways employing the Alexeyev shallow draft submerged foil system, Strela type craft, with surface-piercing trapeze foils, operate in the Gulf of Finland, and together with Kometas and Vikhrs, provide year-round services between ports on the Black Sea. Strelas, visually speaking, are a cross between the PT 20 and PT 50, and have recently been joined on the Leningrad–Tallin route by the gas-turbine powered Typhoon, Russia's first commercial vessel with a fully-submerged foil system.

The Soviet hydrofoil fleet, because of the abundance of waterways throughout the land, is far and away the biggest in the world, with some 8–900 water-buses in service, plus several thousand Volga and similar water-taxis and recreational craft to supply local personal transportation needs.

Emphasis is given by marine research establishments to the furtherance of hydrofoil technology and, if current trends continue, it is anticipated by reliable observers, that the country will become the world's major exporter of this type of craft by the early 1980s. One design alone, the Kometa, a seagoing version of the Meteor, is now in service in Cuba, Italy, Iran, France, Morocco, Poland, Rumania, Bulgaria and Yugoslavia. Demand for these craft is increasing and new models are being introduced with air-stabilisation, improved engines and a V-drive to obviate the characteristic down-by-the stern 'sit' (attitude) of Sormovo designs, increasing the hull clearance height aft. Output is being increased and it is likely that a new yard will be established at

Batumi or another suitable location on the Black Sea to handle exclusively the assembly and modification of this and many other craft for export. Designs likely to be handled by the yard include the Kometa, Voskhod, Nevka and the waterjet-propelled Cyclone a 'stretched', double-decked Kometa, seating 250 passengers.

Anticipating the growing world demand for Russian hydrofoils, a London-based company, Airavia Ltd, is specialising in adapting Sormovo hydrofoils to meet the requirements of the world's marine licensing authorities. During 1974–75, it undertook the modification to UK Department of Trade standards, of three Raketas and a number of Kometas, all of which were issued with British Civil Passenger Operating Certificates. One Raketa was exported to the Philippines, and at the time of writing, two are being operated on the Thames by an associate company, Speed Hydrofoils Ltd.

## Industrial and police uses

The first major oil company to recognise that water transport was at last entering a new era was Shell. Impressed by the speed and comfort of Naveca's PT 20s, Shell's Venezuelan associate, Compania Shell de Venezuela, ordered from Werf Gusto, in Holland, three modified PT 20s to carry oilworkers to and from drilling sites on Lake Maracaibo. The vessels, which began operations in July 1961, were based at a central point, and since the furthest platforms and tenders were only 34 miles away, all drilling locations could be reached within an hour.

The engine room and bridge were re-located in the foreship for improved vision in tropical waters, where frequently there is an influx of driftwood. Tropical conditions were also taken into consideration in the design and installation of the 1,000 bhp MB 820 marine diesel, which was double-supercharged for maximum performance in the hot climate. Within the first twelve months the three craft had accumulated 6,000 hours operational service and carried 95,000 passengers. Shell stated, that as a result of the reduction in pounding experienced in previous crew boats and the quicker service, travel fatigue was greatly reduced.

Later, Rodriquez introduced the RHS 70 and RHS 140 'Hydroils' which feature an open cargo deck aft of the bridge superstructure instead of a passenger saloon. The first of this series, an RHS 70, was supplied to ENI Oil Corporation of Italy, and operates to the company's drilling platforms in the Adriatic.

In 1974, Boeing and Grumman began marketing open-deck utility versions of the Jetfoil and Super Flagstaff for oil rig support and fire-fighting. Boeing stated that a great deal of interest is being shown in 50- and 100-seat crew supply versions of the Jetfoil, which have sufficient cargo capacity and range to support locations 250 nautical miles from the shore.

Another early convert to hydrofoils was the Hessian police force in West Germany, which ordered three PT 3s for water traffic patrols on the Rhine. They discovered that because of their manoeuvrability at high speed, the craft could be navigated in areas thick with ships, motor boats, sailing craft and house-boats without either fear of a collision or of creating a wash to endanger other craft. Foilborne or hullborne, the highest waves and strongest currents created by high tides or storms on the Rhine could be coped with quite safely. Police officers found they could board other vessels in motion with absolutely safety, even when the vessels concerned were large Rhine barges lying in the wake created by their tugs. A further point in the hydrofoil's favour was that when foilborne, other vessels could be overtaken in narrow waters, even at a distance of only four to eight feet, without the wake forcing the hydrofoil to alter course.

## Military hydrofoils

Although military hydrofoils of up to 80 tons displacement and with speeds of up to 50 knots had been designed and built some thirty years earlier, it was not until the mid-1970s that NATO nations began to appreciate their advantages over conventional warships for a number of major missions in modern warfare. Restricted funds, inflation and a general manpower shortage have prompted an increasing number of navies to adopt the 'more and smaller' policy for their sea defences. From the cost/effectiveness viewpoint, the 50-knot multi-duty, seagoing hydrofoil is an attractive investment. It costs far less than the destroyer or frigate it replaces, and besides being much faster, it reduces its speed only slightly in the higher sea-states. Other points in its favour are that it has greater manoeuvrability, its maintenance requirements are generally lower than those of comparable conventional vessels, and its crewing requirements are lower. Armed with anti-ship missiles, even a 60-ton craft can take on a much larger displacement vessel with impunity, and its retractable foils mean that, unlike the larger craft, it can operate totally independently of deepwater anchorages.

Crew comfort in these mini-super-warships of tomorrow should reach a new peak. Seasickness in rough weather in the larger and more sophisticated hydrofoils should all but disappear. The designers, who have successfully computerised the entire flight control system, claim that the magnitude of the vertical and lateral accelerations will compare favourably with those experienced in a medium-range jet airliner. Human reactions to vertical accelerations vary from person to person, but on the whole they are comfortable only within relatively low limits. On conventional patrol boats, accelerations of 10 g. have been recorded, but crews have not been able to tolerate this for long. Generally speaking, humans find that accelerations are perceptible at .01 g, uncomfortable at about 0.1 g, and become intolerable over extended periods at 1 g. According to Boeing, crews operating the PHM in the Mediterranean can expect to find vertical accelerations remaining below 0.1 g at a speed of 45 knots for more than 95 per cent. of the time, while those operating in the Baltic will find them below 0.1 g for 90 per cent. of the time. At the same time, roll and pitch angles are expected to remain below 2 degrees.

Among the purchasers and potential purchasers of the 230-ton Boeing NATO/PHM (Pages 90/91) are the US Navy, the navy of the German Federal Republic and the Italian Navy. The first vessel, the PHM-1, Patrol Hydrofoil (Guided Missile) Pegasus, was delivered to the US Navy in the summer of 1975 and the Navy's planning calls, tentatively, for twenty-four craft to follow. The Federal Republic of Germany plans to buy ten PHMs from Boeing and the Italian Navy one, with another four to six craft being built in Italy. The programme is being watched closely by other NATO countries—Canada, Norway, Denmark, the Netherlands, France and the United Kingdom plus Sweden, Japan and Australia. In Italy, trials of the CNR Alinavi Swordfish —a derivative of the Boeing Tucumcari—have been completed and the Italian Navy plans to order three more.

Other military craft on offer from Western manufacturers include de Havilland Canada's DHC-MP (Maritime Patrol) -100 a multi-duty vessel of 104 tons displacement (Page 88) and a top speed of 50 knots, and Grumman's new Super Flagstaff. The latter, conceived as a high-speed patrol gunboat or missile craft, can be equipped for a number of alternative roles, including anti-submarine warfare search and rescue and fast military transport.

The US Naval Sea Systems Command is currently undertaking the design of larger and faster vessels, one of which, intended for the destroyer escort hydrofoil (DEH) role, will be capable of crossing oceans. The vessel which is in the 1,100–1,300 ton range, would have a top speed at 50 knots, and be available in a number of configurations including a helicopter-equipped ASW ship and an all-purpose weapons platform. One of the companies participating in the development of this project is Boeing. Boeing's Destroyer Escort Hydrofoil design team feels that, without the initiation of any significant new research, an effective hydrofoil escort ship of this size is now feasible.

Unlike the NATO nations, the Soviet Union and later the Warsaw Pact countries, recognised the suitability of hydrofoils for military application soon after World War II. The first hydrofoil vessels to enter service with the Soviet Navy were the 75-ton P 8 class, wooden-hulled torpedo-boats which were equipped with bow foils only and a gas-turbine boost for sprint performance. Later on came the Pchela (Bee), a military derivative of the Strela, which entered service in the mid-1960s and is now in service with the KGB Frontier Police in the Baltic, Black Sea, Caspian and various other sea areas. The craft is equipped with a full range of search and navigation radar and has a speed of about 35 knots. Twenty-five craft are believed to have been built.

China's main production hydrofoil is the Hu Chwan (White Swan) torpedo-boat which has been in production at the Hutang Shipyard Shanghai, since 1966. Sixty or more are in service with the navy of the Chinese People's Republic; another twelve are operating in the Adriatic with the Albanian Navy, and four were supplied to the Pakistan Navy in 1973. The Hu Chwan, in exactly the same way as the Soviet P 8, is based on an earlier displacement torpedo-boat hull to which a bow foil, retractable in this particular case, has been added for increased performance in relatively calm conditions. The foil system comprises a bow subfoil to facilitate take-off, and a trapeze or shallow V main foil set back approximately one-third of the hull length from the bow. At high speed all but the stern of the hull is raised clear of the water. Two 1,100 hp M-50 diesels give the craft a maximum foilborne speed of 55 knots.

One of the latest Eastern bloc military hydrofoils is the Turya class torpedo-boat, the first of which made its debut in the

Eastern Baltic in the spring of 1972. The craft, based on a standard Osa FPB hull, is equipped with a fixed, surface-piercing trapeze foil at the bow only. This increases its speed in relatively calm conditions, improves its seakeeping ability and reduces its wave impact response, which enhances its performance as a weapons platform. The armament of the Osa conversion includes guns and torpedoes and it appears to have been designed for the ASW role.

Baron Hanns von Schertel, who designed and built the world's first military hydrofoils, states that one of the reasons why Western navies failed to adopt foilborne craft earlier is that many senior officers had the idea that they were highly specialised and needed to be supported by highly skilled personnel. As a result it was assumed that exceptional costs would be involved, not to mention high technical risks. But when the operational and maintenance requirements of a modern fast patrol boat (FPB) are compared with those of a naval hydrofoil, it is soon evident that the problems involved are practically identical.

The Supramar design team predicts that in the not too distant future data on projected conventional FPBs will be made available to hydrofoil designers who will then be able to plan a foilborne variant of the vessel, employing existing, proven components. The craft can then be designed to meet a specification almost identical to that of the conventional FPB, but its operational advantages of higher speed, improved range and superior sea-state performance can be utilised to the full without modifying the original requirement.

In the future the hydrofoil is likely to be employed in many different roles, from assault craft and minelayer to convoy escort. Compared with conventional craft of similar size it offers a performance unprecedented in warship design.

# CHAPTER FIVE

# HOVERING HEAVYWEIGHTS

Civil engineering contractors were amongst the first to recognise that, stripped of its cabin and propulsion system, the hovercraft could be transformed into a vehicle capable of carrying heavy loads across marshland and other terrain impassable to normal wheeled vehicles. Unless they are specially designed for multi-terrain operation, wheeled vehicles suffer from ground contact pressures which cause them to bog down, in addition to which their wheels cannot climb over obstructions higher than 0.3 times the wheel radius. The concept of the hovertrailer has existed for a number of years, but it was not until 1969 that sufficient resources had become available to companies within the industry to design and build a prototype.

Work on this type of vehicle was first undertaken by Air Cushion Equipment Ltd, one of the few companies in the world to specialise in the application of air-cushion systems to the industrial and medical fields. Its chairman, Leslie A. Hopkins, was one of the technical group led by Sir Christopher Cockerell at Hovercraft Development Ltd, at Hythe, Southampton, where he specialised in industrial applications. He left the HDL Technical Group (latterly NPL), in April 1968 to found Air Cushion Equipment where he planned to develop his ideas on a variety of industrial ACV devices, from hovertrailers and hover-platforms, to industrial skirts and hoverbeds.

By early 1969, a 7-ton capacity prototype, designated ACE 7, had shown that it was practical to operate a hovertrailer with an average hoverheight of 11–12 in., and ground pressure of about 100 psf across almost any terrain. It had demonstrated, moreover, that valuable farmland could be traversed without damaging the surface. Meadows were crossed without disturbing the flowers, and wet ground, including New Forest peat bogs, was unable to impede its progress. The drawbar pull when fully loaded was only 500 lb, and it was found the vehicle could be manhandled with ease on level surfaces by two men.

Dynamic tests were undertaken at various locations with several kinds of towing vehicles, from low-pressure tracked vehicles of the type used in the Arctic, to old farm tractors. Gradients, ditches, bumps, hard and soft ground, concrete steps and a 30-in. high grass bank were included in the test course, all of which were cleared by the vehicle with ease. Although the tractors were not designed to pull such heavy loads, they showed no tendency to lose traction and their wheels left no marked impression on the terrain.

The standard hovertrailer is based on a rigid, rectangular steel platform, with a strong welded subframe to which a segmented skirt is attached. The vehicle rides on a cushion of air with a working pressure of a fraction of a pound per square in. Lift power is provided by a centrifugal fan coupled to a petrol (gasoline) or diesel power unit mounted at the rear. Special wheels fitted to swinging arms are provided at the rear to give directional control when reversing and on side slopes. Trailers of up to 100 tons capacity can be built by the company and all are designed to be linked together side-by-side to provide a broader base for awkward loads, like pile-drivers, with a high centre of gravity.

In 1970, as a result of an expansion policy at ACE, new associate companies were formed in the United Kingdom and abroad to take on the design, manufacture and sale of industrial hover vehicles. One of the companies was Hovertrailers International Ltd (now UBM Hover Systems Ltd), which was launched under a joint venture agreement between ACE and United Builders Merchants Ltd. Since then, scores of hovertrailers have been designed and built and are being used the world over in widely varying application fields from civil engineering, pipe or cable laying, forestry work, geological and mineral surveying, to agriculture, conservation and drainage schemes.

In conjunction with Hovertrailers, ACE designed and built a system for the recovery of crashed aircraft on behalf of British Airways. This was demonstrated for the first time in March 1970. The system, comprising a number of hover platforms and air bags, can be transported in a standard Boeing 707 air freighter. The advantage of this air-cushion approach is that recovery can be undertaken quickly, regardless of the condition of the ground surface. It is available for all jet aircraft in commercial use, up to the size of the Boeing 747, DC-10 and Concorde.

ACE is also working in conjunction with Global Marine, a large Los Angeles-based exploration, oil, gas and drilling contractor, on a project to float complete oil drilling rigs on air

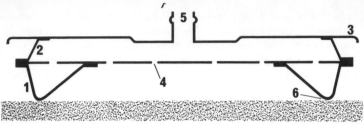

Diagram of a cushion

| | |
|---|---|
| 1 Flexible lip | 4 Cushion air feed holes |
| 2 Suspension | 5 Air supply neck |
| 3 Frame | 6 Air leakage cap |

*Bertin circular pallet for industrial materials handling. The number of individual pallets employed in a handling platform is determined by the function, weight and nature of the load. Three at least must be used on a platform to ensure stability. The cushions are fitted to a chassis with spring clips. Air is fed into the pallet from any suitable industrial compressed air source.*

for use in the Canadian Arctic and Alaska. One of the first developments of this partnership has been the ACT-100, a 100-ton capacity (264-ton auw) amphibious transporter, built in Edmonton, Alberta, in 1971. Five months of Arctic winter trials held on the Great Slave Lake at Yellowknife, Canadian NW Territories, proved extremely successful, with the craft operating at temperatures below —50°F without fault.

The Canadian Ministry of Transport employed the ACT-100 under contract to investigate the feasibility of operating air-cushion ferries on the Mackenzie River highway system between November 1972 and June 1973. Later it was used to carry loads of almost 100 tons over ice, broken-up ice and sea, to an artificial island constructed by Imperial Oil Co. in the Beaufort Sea. The operators reported that they found the vehicle extremely stable and manoeuvrable when travelling over level terrain, slopes, water and over varying thicknesses of ice.

The success of the ACT-100 has led to the design of a completely self-contained, air-cushion supported Arctic Drilling System (ADS) with a gross weight of 3,840 long tons; a 6,000-ton gross weight Arctic marine pipelaying system (AMPS) (Pages 54/55) and an air-cushion ice-breaking attachment for conventional displacement ships heading for ice-bound waters.

The sales and marketing aspects of ACE's and Global Marine's Arctic vehicle designs are handled by Arctic Engineers and

Constructors, a joint venture between Global Marine and Raymond International of New York City.

Another of ACE's associates is Mackley–Ace Ltd, which specialises in the design and construction of hoverplatforms and which also helped incidentally to build the world's first hover-dredger.

During 1974 the company built a 250-ton payload air-cushion transporter in Abu Dhabi for operations in the Arabian Gulf. This is being employed to carry prefabricated sections of a liquid natural gas (LNG) plant from a fabrication site at Abu Dhabi to an installation site at Das Island, a distance of 110 miles.

The use of HDL's industrial skirts by ACE for moving oil storage tanks is now handled through licensed contractors. One of these, Mears Construction Ltd, holds the franchise for the United Kingdom, Western Europe and part of the Middle East. Amongst the company's contracts in 1975 was the resiting of a 700-ton, oil storage tank for Shell Française at their refinery at Pauillac, near Bordeaux. It was the biggest tank ever moved by the hover flotation method. Moreover, while it was being moved the roof was floated on a second cushion of air to reduce the possibilities of damaging it during the resiting. Another organisation which has become increasingly active in the field of air-cushion trailers is the All-Union Oil Machinery Research Institute, Tyumen, West Siberia. Air-cushion oil rig platforms have been under development by the Institutes' Air-Cushion Vehicle Department, headed by V. A. Shibanov, since 1968.

The Tyumen area is rich in oil and petroleum but nearly 80 per cent. of the drilling sites are located amid almost impassable swamps, salt marshes and lakes. By 1968, Shibanov's design group had successfully designed and built the BU-75-VP, a 200-ton hoverplatform, capable of carrying a complete oil rig across tundra, lakes, marshes and snow or water-filled ravines. The vehicle comprises a rectangular, all-metal buoyancy raft with side structures to carry a bag skirt. The derrick, adapted from a standard oil rig, is mounted on the central raft, together with the drilling pump and sundry items of drilling gear. Power is provided by two diesel engines which are employed for drilling at the various sites and for driving the lift fans when moving to fresh locations.

Very much larger ACV rigs with load capacities of up to several thousand tons are reported to be under construction. Engineers at the Institute are also developing a range of hovertrailers similar in overall configuration to those built by Hover-trailers International Ltd. The smallest is a vehicle of 6 tonnes, powered by a single gas-turbine driving twin axial-flow fans for cushion lift. Next in size is the 40-tonne capacity PVP-40, powered by a single diesel engine driving two centrifugal fans, and the largest is a vehicle with a payload of 60-tonnes, with axial fans, like those of the smaller craft, driven by an industrial-ised gas-turbine. The Institute's air-cushion supported oil rig, was the first vehicle of its type in the world.

Even more unorthodox than some of the ACV trailers and platforms are their 'tugs'. In Poland one agricultural hovertrailer employs a horse or farmhand for propulsion, but surpassing this even for sheer novelty is the Sikorsky S-55 helicopter employed in the Canadian Far North by the National Research Council of Canada for experiments with the 15-ton Hover-Jak HJ-15. According to the Council, which is concerned with limiting damage to sensitive tundra, the helicopter may mean the difference between operating a three-month and a ten-month work period during the year. The S-55 can tow the fully-laden hovertrailer at speeds up to 20 mph.

Yet another unusual tractor is the MVP-3, a vehicle designed by V. A. Shibanov's group at Tyumen, West Siberia. It combines crawler propulsion with air-cushion lift and has a flexible skirt between its crawler tracks.

No survey of the industrial applications of the air cushion would be complete without reference to the CEGB Heavy Load Transporters designed and built initially by Vickers Ltd and later by BHC. The weight of large transformers for generator stations has increased to the 300–500-ton range. On a number of occasions the Central Electricity Generating Board has been involved in heavy expense in order to strengthen and rebuild bridges to accept these loads when no alterantive route has been available. However, by providing an air cushion under the centre section of an existing transporter, a high proportion of the trans-porter's load is uniformly distributed over the area enclosed by the cushion. By changing the concentrated tire loads to uniformly distributed air pressure loads, the peak stresses are reduced inside a bridge or roadway, increasing the total load that can be carried. The savings in bridge strengthening costs are estimated by the Central Electricity Generating Board as being in excess of £1,500,000—added to which drivers of other vehicles have not been subjected to the inconvenience of bridge reconstruction work.

One of the systems under development by ACE is designed to support a 350-ton transformer mounted on a fourteen-axle girder trailer. The cushion system, powered by two small gas-turbines, develops a pressure of 5 psi, giving an axle relief of 125 tons, significantly reducing the stresses in the bridge. Equipment of this type has been used at hundreds of bridge locations. Some journeys have required the use of ACV trailers at a single bridge, others at no fewer than twenty-seven locations.

At the opposite end of the scale of the trailers employed to transport giant transformers, are the compact air pallets used in an increasing number of countries to move major items of generating gear into position inside power stations. Air bearing cells are invariably circular and have a flexible diaphragm sealed around the circumference at the base. Compressed air from a normal factory airline source or mobile compressor inflates the diaphragm, passing the air down through small holes to the space below. The thin layer of air between the membrane and the floor forms a frictionless air film which 'floats' the load, allowing it to be moved in any horizontal direction by a force only 1/1000 of the weight of the load.

Air bearings are employed for literally hundreds of industrial applications, from assembly lines for crawler tractors to rotating Boeing 747 Jumbo jets during pre-flight testing and compass calibration. One of the most ambitious applications is to be found in Honolulu, where Rolair Systems Inc., has employed air bearings to vary the seating configurations of a new 28,000-seat stadium. The stadium comprises four 7,000-seat sections, and the air bearings are employed to rotate each through a 45 degree arc to provide ideal patterns for either football, baseball, basketball games or stage shows.

Medical science has benefited from the air-cushion principle, too. One major development has been the hoverbed, for the treatment of patients with severe burns, pioneered by Hovercraft Development Ltd. When the patient is placed on the bed, two rows of pockets, based on the segmented skirts used on hovercraft, form a seal along the sides of the body, and then fall away beneath it. The body is left solely supported on air, though normally the head is supported on a pillow. The seal automatically conforms to any size of patient and follows any movement of the patient. The air unit is housed in a four-wheeled trailer outside the ward. A number of these units have been installed in hospitals throughout the United Kingdom.

# CHAPTER SIX

# AIR-CUSHION AIRCRAFT

In size, shape and application, the giant Lockheed Spanloader and the diminutive, Australian-built Jindivik are a world apart. The Spanloader, one of a new generation of heavy lift freighters, is expected to be capable of carrying a payload of 560,000 pounds non-stop from the USA to the Middle East. In contrast, the Jindivik is a 21-ft span, unmanned weapons target with a loaded weight of only 3,500 pounds. Closer examination, however, shows that the Spanloader and the latest version of the Jindivik do have one major feature in common—an air-cushion system (ACLS).

In the past, an aircraft had either wheels, skis or floats, or possibly a combination of a monohull and wheels. Never before has a single system been available that combines the functional capabilities of them all. The system minimises airstrip requirements and enables aircraft to take-off and land from any flat unprepared surfaces—open fields, open water, ice, snow, marshland, sand and dirt. It also permits aircraft to make safe and controlled crosswind landings and take-offs.

Even more, it will enable the new range of giant freight planes like the Spanloader and the Bertin Cygne series of 1,000-ton-plus free-flying/surface-effect vehicles to take-off and land with far heavier loads than can be borne by conventional multi-wheel undercarriages. These large freight planes will be able to operate independently of conventional airports, relieving some of the pressure imposed on them as world air traffic builds up. Services could then be operated to many parts of the world where the cost of constructing a conventional airport to international size and standards would be prohibitive, but where a suitable stretch of land could be prepared by bulldozers. Runways and taxiways would be eliminated and almost the only form of construction necessary would be in the provision of aprons for loading and offloading freight.

Considerable interest is being shown in the employment of air-cushion aircraft in the Arctic, since they would be capable of servicing areas which cannot be reached by tracked vehicles, ACVs or dog sleds. ACLS-equipped STOL aircraft would fly over the mountain ranges, broken ice floes and pressure ridges and land on any suitable strip of flat or relatively flat ice surface adjacent to the site being serviced to deliver its load.

The first successful air-cushion aircraft was a Lake LA-4 single-engine light amphibian, conceived at Bell Aerospace under the direction of T. D. Earl, who began his ACLS experiments at Avro Canada in the early 1950's on the Avrocar vertical take-off fighter. The LA-4 ACLS consists of a doughnut-shaped bag or trunk attached to the LA-4's spray rail. The trunk is fabricated from multiple layers of stretch nylon cloth for strength, natural rubber for elasticity and coated with neoprene for environmental stability. An axial fan, powered by a separate engine, forces air into the trunk, inflating it to a depth of 2 ft (0.60 m.). The air escapes into the cushion through thousands of tiny jet nozzles on the bag's underside. In deflated condition, the trunk retracts tightly against the hull because of its inherent elasticity.

On landing, six brake skids on the underside of the trunk are brought into contact with the landing surface by inflating pneumatic pillows. For parking on land or water, a lightweight bladder inside the trunk seals the airjets, thus supporting the aircraft at rest on land or providing it with buoyancy to keep it afloat on water. Pilots of the LA-4 agree that, in general, on all improved surfaces, ACLS is easier to control than a wheeled undercarriage, and its performance on surfaces where the use of conventional wheels is impossible gives no problems. They state that the stability of the ACLS to make a safe and controlled landing in high crosswinds is outstanding. It is also 'more forgiving' to pilots approaching at the wrong landing attitude and at higher descent rates at touchdown than a conventional landing gear.

The LA-4 performed its first take-off and landing in September 1969 in 25 mph winds on Lake Erie. It required only 650 ft of water for take-off and 250 ft for landing; then demonstrated its amphibious capability by taxiing ashore.

In November 1970, a joint United States/Canadian programme was launched with the objective of demonstrating through ground and flight tests the capabilities of an ACLS-equipped military transport aircraft. De Havilland Aircraft of Canada Ltd modified an XC-8A Buffalo STOL transport aircraft for the ACLS installation; United Aircraft of Canada Ltd developed two ST6F-70 gas-turbine fan systems to supply air to the ACLS and Bell supplied the trunk system.

The inflatable trunk, which is an enlarged version of that used on the experimental LA-4, was completed in February 1973. Flight tests began in mid-1974 and were still in progress at the time of writing. The two ACLS engines are mounted one each side of the fuselage, beneath the wings, in a similar way to the jet-assisted take-off bottles (JATO) employed on a number of carrier-based utility and 'strike' aircraft to shorten their take-off run when carrying extra-heavy loads. Either of the two auxiliary engines can be used to operate the on-board compressor in the event of one failing, and after take-off, they can be shut down or used to provide additional propulsive thrust. Wing-tip floats are fitted for overwater operation, each float having a fibre-glass spring skid beneath it to prevent excessive roll and to protect the propellers while taxiing over land. Finally, the standard Buffalo propellers have been modified to give the pilot direct control of the blade angles. This provides him with asymmetric power and, by changing the blade settings differentially, he has more positive directional control while taxiing. He brakes the craft by reversing the propeller pitch and employing the braking pillows (skids) described earlier. The larger air-cushion trunk enables the XC-8A to cross ditches 9–10-ft wide and clear 18-in. tree stumps and boulders. The success of the ACLS systems on the LA-4 and XC-8A is expected to lead to a much greater demand for this type of undercarriage in future for both commercial and military applications.

The Jindivik study, awarded to Bell by the USAF in 1974, has the objective of employing the ACLS as a means of discarding the rocket-assisted take-off units or launch aircraft, launching cradles, and recovery parachutes which are an expensive but inevitable feature of unmanned target vehicle operation today. On the Jindivik, air is bled from the Viper gas-turbine to inflate the landing trunk and a more rapid breaking process is used, but otherwise the system, though smaller, is almost identical to that of the XC-8A.

A preliminary study contract undertaken by Bell in conjunction with several other major US companies showed that by employing a surface-effect, take-off and landing system (SETOL), a single naval aircraft would have the capability of performing a variety of roles formerly requiring a land-based aircraft, a carrier-based aircraft and a seaplane. The roles included close support, search and rescue, logistics support, amphibious assault cover, reconnaissance, and the transfer of equipment and personnel between ships on the move.

Development of ACLS systems in the Soviet Union is being encouraged by one of their most senior aircraft designers, Robert Oro di Bartini, who built the first aircraft with a completely retractable undercarriage in the USSR in 1933. Bartini, former head of the Scientific Research Institute of the Soviet Civil Air Fleet, forecasts that ACLS gear will possibly have replaced conventional wheeled undercarriages on a great number of aircraft types by the end of the century.

# CHAPTER SEVEN

# TOMORROW'S SUPER TRAINS

If today's 'tracked skimmer' concepts prove successful, tomorrow's inter-city trains will carry their passengers from city centre to city centre far quicker than anyone could hope to travel by jet airliner.

One of the major goals of the ground transportation authorities in France, the USA, West Germany and Japan, is the development of a tracked transit system capable of moving passengers and freight over distances of up to 500 miles at 300 mph. Integrated with this would be automatically controlled train systems serving city centres and urban areas. Underground, elevated or ground level guideways could be provided for these commuter systems and would be adaptable to passenger flows ranging from a minimum of 1,000 to a maximum of 20,000 per hour during peak commuting periods.

The growing interest in high-speed, tracked transport concepts is due to the rapid deterioration in railway services and the noise, jams and pollution caused by other forms of conveyance. According to Dr Howard T. Coffey, of the Stanford Research Institute, California (which has been working on High Speed Ground Transportation Systems for the US Government), in 1969 travel in the USA was undertaken in 84 million cars, 88,000 buses, 16,000 railway carriages, 1,500 four-engined aircraft, 120,000 aircraft with fewer than four engines and other vehicles. Between them, the vehicles and their operators killed 50,000 people in that year, injured another 4 million and added significantly to air pollution, which in some of the world's major cities, is now approaching critical proportions.

Because of this and the gradual choking of the metropolitan areas by road traffic, it is recognised that any attempt to perpetuate today's totally inadequate transport arrangements could only lead to a catastrophic situation long before the turn of the century when the demands on it will be far heavier. In the USA, for example, 1969's population will probably have doubled by the year 2,000.

Ground transportation experts are convinced that many of the present problems could be overcome simply by introducing a fast, comfortable, pollution-free train system, capable of winning over car drivers and airline passengers on the basis of convenience, comfort, speed and cost. The ever-increasing price of fossil fuels is likely to become a major incentive. At the target speed of 300 mph, journey times would be exceptionally fast: London to Glasgow would take eighty minutes, Paris to Berlin, one hour fifty minutes and New York to Central Washington, a bare forty minutes. At the same time all the disadvantages of inter-city air travel would be avoided, particularly its susceptibility to bad weather, the traffic delays en route to the airport, and the necessity to observe check-in times. Compared with medium-distance jet airliners, the services would be more frequent, and the journey would be covered in almost complete silence. In Japan, it is hoped to have such a system in operation by the early 1980's.

In the tracked skimmer field at present there are already two contenders, both of which are sufficiently attractive to draw passengers back to the railways in their thousands. These are the tracked air-cushion vehicle (TACV) and the magnetically-levitated vehicle (MAGLEV). Tracked air-cushion vehicles are supported and guided on their concrete guideways by air cushions surrounded by skirts. Their propulsion can be by either gas-turbine, propeller-turbine or linear induction motor.

Magnetically-levitated vehicles are normally raised and propelled by magnetic fields only. Experiments have shown that magnetic levitation is capable of suspending vehicles at 300 mph (483 km/h) and development is now being concentrated on two systems. The first, employs the attractive force between a controlled electromagnet on board the vehicle and a ferromagnetic rail. The second utilises superconducting magnets on board the vehicle and the currents are induced in a guideway. As the vehicle's magnet passes over the aluminium-clad guideway, eddy currents are induced in the coils, leading to a stable repulsive levitation force which lifts and centres the vehicle in its channel-shaped guideway. At present, it is felt that neither of the two magnetic levitation systems has proved greatly superior to the other, nor have they shown any great advantage over air-cushion suspension systems. Moreover, a recent study in the United States has indicated that the ram air-cushion suspension concept has the potential for lower energy consumption than either the earlier tracked air-cushion vehicle or MAGLEV concepts.

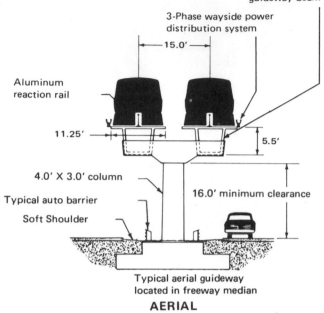

Prestressed concrete
guideway beam

3-Phase wayside power
distribution system

|← 15.0' →|

Aluminum
reaction rail

11.25'

5.5'

4.0' X 3.0' column

16.0' minimum clearance

Typical auto barrier

Soft Shoulder

Typical aerial guideway
located in freeway median

**AERIAL**

*Types of guideway planned in the United States for the Aerotrain 150 mph
Airport Access Series.* (See also facing page.)

TACVs have been under development for nearly seventy-five
years. The first proposal was that of an eminent French engineer,
Charles Theryc, who between 1902 and 1915 obtained a number
of patents on the use of air for a sliding-railway. In 1922 a Mr
F. G. Trask of North Dakota, USA, patented a sliding-railway
in which the air employed to support the train was also for
propulsion. In 1927, another American, Dr Andrew A. Kucher,
a Ford Motor Company vice-president, introduced his Levacar
concept. Kucher recognised that the limiting factor in improving
the speed of ground transportation is the wheel, and to overcome
this, he proposed a principle of 'levitation' in which vehicles
would glide on a thin film of air at speeds higher than those
possible through the use of wheels.

One of Kucher's concepts, the air-propelled Levacar X-5, was

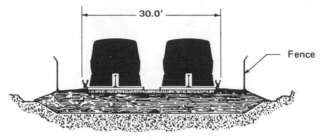

**SURFACE**

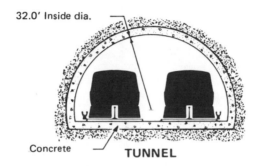

32.0' Inside dia.

Concrete

**TUNNEL**

designed to operate between cities 90–100 miles apart at 150 mph. Ford is still active in this field today and handles a number of US government research contracts. The TACV offers several major advantages over existing railway systems. The tracks, for example, are relatively cheap to build and would be mounted on slim pylons and therefore create relatively little disturbance to the areas beneath. Also, the vehicles would not subject the tracks to the loads and vibrations generated by normal wheeled carriages, and would be practically noiseless. Relatively small vehicle units would be operated in order to provide flexibility, and as very high frequency services would be introduced at peak periods— between ten and twelve an hour—they would virtually dispense with the need for timetables. Initially, inter-city vehicles would be able to attain 200–300 mph and the suburban vehicles 50–120 mph, but higher speeds are forecast.

In France, the development of the Bertin Aerotrain TACV system started in 1965, and has culminated in the construction of the I-80, a medium-range vehicle designed for the Orleans–Paris

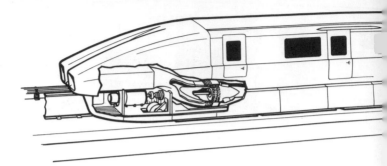

line. The first leg of the line, a track 11.5 miles (18.5 km) long was completed in July 1969. By May 1974, the I-80 Aerotrain had completed more than 850 hours of operating, logging more than 30,000 miles and carrying 13,000 passengers. Designed originally for airscrew propulsion, it has recently been equipped with a 15,000-lb thrust Pratt & Whitney JT8D-11 turbofan which has increased its speed to 250 mph (426 km/h). During tests, speed, acceleration and braking characteristics have confirmed expectations and passengers have been enthusiastic about the comfort of the ride.

In November 1969, Société de l'Aérotrain formed a US subsidiary, Aérotrain-Systems Inc., to build and market Aerotrains in the United States and Mexico. The company, which is operated jointly by Rohr Industries, Bertin et Cie and Société de l'Aérotrain, has supplied its first prototype to the US Department of Transportation's Federal Railroad Administration for trials at the Department's test centre, near Pueblo, Colorado.

Also undergoing trials at the test centre are the Grumman TLRV, powered by three JT15D turbofans, and the AiResearch Manufacturing Co's Linear Induction Motor Research Vehicle (LIMRV). All three vehicles have played an important part in the Department of Transportation's High Speed Ground Transportation Programme, the objective of which is to provide, by the late 1970's technical information on whether a TLV

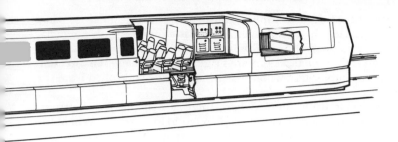

*The Rohr-built M-60 Aerotrain prototype is propelled by a linear induction motor and rides on a Bertin air-cushion suspension system. The vehicle operates at 150 m.p.h. on an inverted 'Tee' track and is controlled by computer. The driver monitors the track, front and rear, through a closed-circuit television.*

system is a suitable method for augmenting present transportation systems.

In Western Germany, Krauss–Maffei and Messerschmitt–Bolkow–Blohm have joined forces to devise a new transport system having three characteristics:

> connection of the high density centres of industry and population in the Federal Republic;
>
> facilities to transport trucks, cars and containers, in order to relieve the freeways and highways;
>
> straight-to-destination service, without interim stops and vehicle changes.

After intensive studies, a rapid transit system travelling at up to 312 mph (500 km/h) with magnetic track guidance and propulsion was found to be most favourable.

The companies are now concentrating on the development of the Transrapid, a 148-ft long vehicle, which, dependant upon internal configuration, will carry passengers, cars, general and containerised freight at 312 mph (500 km/h). Payload of the standard Transrapid will be 25 metric tons. Full-width clam-shell doors will be provided at both ends of the vehicle to permit the straight-through loading of vehicles and containers. The first section of a national test facility to test the prototype is due to be completed in 1977.

Krauss–Maffei is also conducting a series of tests with a

prototype of its 38 mph Transurban short-distance tracked system, which, like the larger vehicle is equipped with magnetic support, guidance and propulsion systems. One feature of major interest is that the track employs rigid points, changes in direction being accomplished by magnets which can be controlled from the vehicle.

On major traffic lines, where there is demand for transport, several of the vehicles can be connected to form trains. Where the major line branches off to serve suburban areas, the trains are automatically divided to form individual vehicles. Each vehicle is programmed for a specific line. At the time of departure, the passenger picks the vehicle that will serve his or her destination. In this way the need to change vehicles is avoided along the major arteries of a network.

Numerous other high-speed ground transportation concepts are likely to be built and tested before the 'perfect' system comes to light. But one thing is certain. Railways, in much the same way as water transport, will have taken on a totally different appearance by the end of the century.

# GLOSSARY OF ACV AND HYDROFOIL TERMS

**ACV**  see air-cushion vehicle.

**auw**  all-up weight

**actuator**  unit designed to translate operator or computer instructions into controlled mechanical action. Energy is transferred via the actuator to control surfaces mechanically, hydraulically, pneumatically or electrically

**aerodynamic lift**  lift created by the forward speed of a vehicle due to the difference in pressure between upper and lower surfaces

**Aerofoil boat**  name given by Dr A. M. Lippisch to his range of aerodynamically supported air-cushion vehicles

**aéroglisseur (French)**  generic term for air-cushion vehicles of all types. See *Naviplane*

**aeroplane foil (airplane configuration)**  system in which the main foil is located forward of the centre of gravity to support 75 per cent. to 85 per cent. of the load, with an auxiliary foil, supporting the remainder, located aft

**aerostatic lift**  lift created by a self-generated cushion of pressurised air

**Aérotrain**  name given by M. Jean Bertin to a range of tracked air-cushion vehicle designs under development jointly in France by Société de l'Aérotrain and in the USA by Rohr Corporation

**air-cushion**
**vehicle**
a vehicle capable of being operated so that its weight, including its payload, is totally or significantly supported on a continuously generated cushion of pressurised air. The air cushion is produced by a fan or aerodynamic ram effect and is usually contained beneath the vehicle's structure by flexible skirts or sidewalls. The term is generally employed in the United States to refer to amphibious craft only. The term *surface effect vehicle* is the most general description of the various concepts and includes all types—waterborne, landborne and amphibious. The term *surface effect ship* (*SES*) refers to large surface effect craft limited to waterborne operations only. There are two main types of air-cushion vehicles, those supported by a self-generated cushion of air and those dependant upon forward speed to develop lift. The former are known as 'aerostatic', and the latter, 'aerodynamic'. Most aerodynamic machines are of the wing-in-ground-effect or Ekranoplan type. See *Hovercraft*

**air entry**
entry of air from the atmosphere that raises the low pressures created by the water flowing over a foil's cambered upper surface, greatly reducing lift. Also known as ventilation

**air gap; also**
**hover gap**
distance between the lowest component of the vehicle's understructure and the surface when riding on its cushion

**air gap area**
area through which air is able to leak from a cushion. (Circumference times effective air gap)

**air pallet**
air cushion supported load-carrying structure, which bleeds a continuous low pressure volume of air between the structure and the reaction surface, creating an air film, which essentially eliminates friction between the structure and the surface

**angle of attack**   angle between the mean chord line of a foil and the flow

**angle of incidence**   angle of the mean chord line of a hydrofoil in relation to the fixed struts or hull

**axial-flow lift fan**   a lift fan generating an airflow that is parallel to the axis of rotation

**ballast system**   system for transferring water or fuel between tanks to adjust fore and aft trim by changing weight distribution

**beam**   measurement across a hull at a given point. Usually refers to the maximum value

**bridge**   elevated part of the superstructure, from which a craft (or ship) is navigated and steered (conned)

**bulkheads**   vertical partitions, either transverse or longitudinal, which divide or sub-divide a hull

**canard foil system**   foil system in which the main foil of wide span is located near the stern, aft of the centre of gravity, and bears about 65 per cent. of the weight, while a small central foil, carrying the remainder of the weight, is placed at the bow

**captured air bubble craft; also sidewall vessel**   expression originated in the USA for a vessel in which the cushion (or air bubble) is contained by rigid sidewalls and flexible bow and stern skirts. See *Air-cushion vehicle*

**surface-effect ship cavitation**   a phenomenon caused by the formation of vapour bubbles due to decreased pressure at high speed on the upper surface of a foil or the back of a propeller's blades at high speeds, and falling into two categories, unstable and stable. Non-stable cavities or cavitation bubbles of aqueous vapour form near the foil's leading edge and extend downstream expanding and collapsing. At the points of collapse positive localised pressure peaks may rise to as high as 20,000 psi, causing serious erosion and pitting of the metal. Cavitation also creates an unstable water flow over the foils which results in abrupt changes in lift thereby causing discomfort. Foil sections are now being developed which either delay the onset of cavitation by reduced camber, thinner sections, or sweepback, or if the craft is required to operate at supercavitating speeds, stabilise cavitation to provide a smooth transition between sub-cavitating and super-cavitating speeds

**centrifugal flow lift fan**    a lift fan that generates an airflow at right angles to the axis of rotation

**chord**    measurement between the leading and trailing edges of a foil section

**classification; also certification**    waterborne and amphibious craft for commercial use are classified for insurance purposes by type and place of construction, in the manner of the registration system started in the City of London by Edward Lloyd, and continued since 1760 by Lloyd's Register of Shipping. In addition classification societies now include Registro Italiano Navale, Germanischer Lloyd, Det Norske Veritas, and the American Bureau of Shipping and the Japanese Ministry of Transport. A classification society's surveyors make a detailed examination of craft certified by them at regular intervals to ensure their condition complies with the particular society's requirements. Certification, which is essentially a license to operate is provided by regulatory organisations such as the US Coast Guard and, in the United Kingdom, the Department of Trade. It covers not only approval for safety in design, but also inspection of vessels for compliance during construction and throughout its operating life for manning, maintenance, safety, equipment standards and operational aspects. In some countries such as the United States, it represents an almost continuous liaison with the regulatory agency to assure compliance through-out the operational life of the vessel

**contour, to**    the motion of an air-cushion vehicle or hydrofoil when following a wave profile

**craft**    ships, boats, air-cushion vehicles and hydrofoils of all types, regardless of size

**cushion**    volume of higher than ambient air pressure trapped beneath the structure of a vehicle and its supporting surface causing the vehicle to be supported at some distance from the ground

**cushion-seal**    air curtains, sidewalls, skirts, water-jets or other means employed to contain or seal an air cushion reducing to a minimum, the leakage of trapped air

**diesel engine**    internal combustion engine in which air is first drawn into the cylinder and compressed so tightly that the heat generated is sufficient to ignite the oil which is subsequently injected

**drag**    1) ACVs—aerodynamic and hydrodynamic resistances caused by aerodynamic profile, gain of momentum of air needed for cushion gener-ation, wave-making, wetting or skirt contact
2) hydrofoils—hydrodynamic resistances result-ing from wave-making, frictional drag due to the viscosity of the water, the total wetted surface and induced drag from the foils and trans-mission shafts and their supporting struts and structure

**Ekranoplan**    Russian term based on 'ekran', a screen or curtain, and 'plan', the principal supporting surface of an aeroplane. Employed almost exclusively to describe types of ACVs in the

Soviet Union raised above their supporting surfaces by dynamic lift. Western equivalent, wing-in-ground-effect machines (WIG) and aerodynamic ram-wing

**fences**          small partitions placed at short intervals along the upper and lower surfaces of a foil in the direction of the flow to prevent air ventilation passing down to destroy the lift

**foilborne**          a hydrofoil is foilborne when the hull is raised completely out of the water and wholly supported by lift from its foils

**foil systems**          foils in current use are generally either *surface-piercing, submerged* or *semi-submerged*. A number of craft have hybrid systems with a combination of submerged and surface-piercing foils, recent examples being the Supramar PT 150 and the De Havilland FHE-400

**following sea**          a sea following the same or similar course to that of the craft

**frames**          the structure of vertical ribs or girders to which a vessel's outside plates are attached. For identification purposes, the frames are numbered consecutively, starting aft

**freeboard**          depth of the exposed or free side of a hull between the water level and the freeboard deck. The degree of freeboard permitted is marked by load lines

**free power turbine**          a gas-turbine on which the power-turbine is on a separate shaft from the compressor and its turbine

**full hover**          expression used to describe the condition of an ACV when it is at its design hoverheight

**gas-turbine**          turbine rotated by expanding gases

**gas-turbine engine**     engine generally comprising a rotary air compressor, combustion chamber(s), a gas-turbine and an exhaust

**ground-effect machine**     early generic term for surface effect vehicle. Does not usually have water-tight integrity

**head sea**     a sea approaching from the direction steered

**heave**     vertical motion of a craft in response to waves

**heel**     to incline or list in a transverse direction while under way

**hoverbarge**     fully buoyant, shallow-draught hovercraft built for freight carrying. Can be either self-propelled or towed

**hovercraft**     1) originally a name for craft using the patented peripheral jet principle invented by Sir Christopher Cockerell, in which the air cushion is generated and contained by a jet of air exhausted downward and inward from a nozzle at the periphery at the base of the vehicle.
2) classification in the USA for skirted plenum chamber and annular jet-designs.
3) in the British Hovercraft Act 1968, a hovercraft is defined as a vehicle which is designed to be supported when in motion wholly or partly by air expelled from the vehicle to form a cushion of which the boundaries include the ground, water or other surface beneath the vehicle

**hoverpallet**     see *Air pallet*

**hover height**     vertical height between the hard structure of an ACV and the supporting surface when a vehicle is cushionborne

**hover-platform**     non self-propelled hovercraft designed primarily to convey heavy loads across terrain impassable to wheeled and tracked vehicles under load

**hovertrailer** a steel structure platform around which is fitted a flexible segmented skirt, cushion lift being provided by fans driven by petrol or diesel engines on the platform. The system devised by Air Cushion Equipment Ltd and Hovertrailers International Ltd is designed to increase the load capacity of tracked and wheeled vehicles many times. In cases where it is impossible for a tow vehicle to operate, the trailer can be winched

**hump speed** critical intermediate speed at which the curve on a graph of wave-making drag begins to diminish and the rate of acceleration rapidly increases with no increase in power

**hydrofoils** small wings, almost identical in section to those of an aircraft, and designed to generate lift when moved through water. Since water has a density some 815 times that of air, the same lift as an aeroplane wing is obtained for only 1/815 of the area (at equal speeds)

**inclined shaft** a marine drive shaft used in small V-foil and shallow-draught submerged foil craft, with only a limited foilborne hull clearance above the mean water level. The shaft is generally short and inclined at about 12–14 degrees to the horizontal to avoid propeller cavitation. On larger craft, designed for operation in higher waves, the need to fly at greater hull clearances necessitates alternative drive arrangements such as the V-drive and Z-drive, the water jet system or even air propulsion

**integrated lift propulsion system** an ACV lift and propulsion system operated by common power source. The transmission and power-sharing system allows variation in the division of power

**lift fan** a fan used to supply air under pressure to an air cushion, and/or to form curtains

**lift off**  an ACV is said to lift off when it rises from the ground supported by its air cushion

**multi-cell skirt**  system devised by M. Jean Bertin, employing a number of separate flexible skirts for his system of individually-fed, multiple air cushions

**naviplane**  passenger-carrying amphibious ACVs designed in France by Société Bertin & Cie, in conjunction with Société D'Etudes et le Développment des Aéroglisseurs Marin (SEDAM)

**orbital motion**  orbital or circular motion of the water particles forming waves. The circular motion decreases in radius with increasing depth. It is the peculiar sequence of the motion that causes the illusion of wave translation

**pitch**  rotation or oscillation of the hull about a transverse axis in a seaway. Also angle of air or water propeller blades to the flow

**pitch angle**  pitch angle a craft adopts in relation to a horizontal datum

**platform, to**  approximately level flight of a hydrofoil over waves of a height less than the calm water hull clearance

**plenum**  space or air chamber beneath or surrounding a lift fan or fans through which air under pressure is distributed to a skirt system

**plenum chamber cushion system**  most simple of all air-cushion concepts. Cushion pressure is maintained by pumping air continuously into a recessed base without the use of a peripheral jet curtain

**'plough in'**  a bow down attitude resulting from the bow part of the skirt contacting the surface and progressively building up a drag tending to force the craft to nose under. Unless controlled this can lead to a serious loss of stability and possibly an overturning moment

**puff ports**       variable apertures in a skirt system or cushion supply ducting through which air can be expelled to assist control at low speeds by producing lateral motion or rotation

**roll**             oscillation or rotation of a hull about a longitudinal axis

**roll attitude**    angle of roll craft adopts relative to a longitudinal datum

**SES**              surface effect ship. Term used in the USA for a ship-size, sea-going air-cushion vehicle or hovercraft employing rigid sidewalls integral to the hull structure and flexible seals fore and aft to contain the air cushion

**SEV**              surface-effect vehicle. Currently used in the USA to describe amphibious air-cushion vehicles. In the Soviet Union, the term is employed to describe large sea- or ocean-going wing-in-ground-effect machines

**sea-state**        a quantitative scale of sea conditions classified from state 1, smooth, to state 8, precipitous, produced by wind duration, fetch and velocity, and statistically determined wave heights, wave length, period and velocity

**skirt**            fabric extension hung between an ACV's metal structure and the surface. Provides increased obstacle and overwave clearance capability for a small air gap clearance and therefore reduced power requirement

**skirt, bag**       simple skirt design consisting of an inflated bag

**skirt shifting**   control system in which movement of the centre of area of the cushion is achieved by shifting the skirt along one side, which has the effect of tilting the craft. Pitch and roll trim can be adjusted by this method

**sidewall vessel**   surface effect watercraft with its cushion air contained between immersed sidewalls or skegs and transverse air curtains or skirts fore and aft. Stability is provided by the buoyancy of the sidewalls and their planning forces

**significant wave height**   sea waves are composed of different frequencies and have different wave heights. A wave with the leading frequency and energy content is called the significant wave. It is from this wave that the significant wave height is measured. Statistically defined as the average of the one-third highest waves

**split foil**   main foil with its area divided into two, either to facilitate retraction, or to permit the location of the control surfaces well outboard, where foil control and large roll correcting forces can be applied for small changes in lift

**stability skirt**   transverse or longitudinal skirt dividing an air cushion so as to restrict cross-flow within the cushion and increase pitch or roll stability

**submerged foil system**   foil system employing totally submerged lifting surfaces. The depth of foil submergence and craft stability is controlled by mechanical, electronic or pneumatic control systems which direct activators to alter the angle of incidence of the foils or flaps attached to them to provide stability and control

**super-cavitating foil**   a general classification given to foils designed to operate efficiently at high speeds while fully cavitated

**surface effect ship**   see *SES* and *Air-cushion vehicle*

**surface effect vehicle**    see *Air-cushion vehicle*

**TLACV**    track-laying air-cushion vehicle. Air-cushion vehicle employing caterpillar- or tank-like tracks for propulsion. The air cushion and its seals may be located between the flexible tracks as in the case of the Soviet MVP-3 series, or it can take the form of a broad belt or track that loops around the complete air cushion

**take-off speed**    speed at which the hull of a hydrofoil craft is raised clear of the water

**tandem foils**    foil system in which the area of the forward foils is approximately equal to that of the aft foils

**thruster**    controlled aperture through which air can be expelled to assist control at low speeds. Also applied to small ducted fans or even water propellers used exclusively to aid directional control

**trans-cavitating foil**    foil designed for smooth transition from fully wetted to supercavitating flow. By loading the tip more highly than the root, cavitation is first induced at the foil's tip, then extends spanwise over the foil to the roots as speed increases. This provides for cavitation conditions along the foil throughout the transition speed range

**transverse framing**    hull reinforcing frames running athwartships, from side-to-side, instead of in a fore and aft direction

**trim**    ACV and hydrofoil hull attitude relative to the line of flight

**variable-pitch propeller**    a propeller with blades which can rotate about their longitudinal axis to provide forward or reverse thrust for control and optimum performace

**wave height**  vertical distance from wave trough to crest

**winged hull**  alternative name given by Dr Alexander M. Lippisch to his range of aerodynamic ram-wing machines. See also *Aerofoil boat* and *Wing-in-ground-effect*

**wing-in-ground-effect**  an aerodynamic-type air-cushion vehicle which depends upon forward speed in order to develop lift. At speed lifting forces are generated both by the wing and an induced dynamic cushion of air built up between the vehicle and the surface

**yaw angle**  rotation or oscillation of a craft about a vertical axis

**Z-drive**  a drive system normally employed on hydrofoils to transmit power from the engine in the hull to the screw. Power is transmitted through a horizontal shaft leading to a bevel gear over the stern, then via a vertical shaft and a second bevel gear to a horizontal propeller shaft, thus forming a 'Z' shape

# INDEX

Figures in **bold** refer to plate numbers